THE
VALUE
INVESTORS

THE
VALUE
INVESTORS

Lessons from the World's Top Fund Managers

RONALD W. CHAN

WILEY

John Wiley & Sons Singapore Pte. Ltd.

Other Wiley Editorial Offices
John Wiley & Sons, 111 River Street, Hoboken, NJ 07030, USA
John Wiley & Sons, The Atrium, Southern Gate, Chichester, West Sussex, P019 8SQ, United Kingdom
John Wiley & Sons (Canada) Ltd., 5353 Dundas Street West, Suite 400, Toronto, Ontario, M9B 6HB, Canada
John Wiley & Sons Australia Ltd., 42 McDougall Street, Milton, Queensland 4064, Australia
Wiley-VCH, Boschstrasse 12, D-69469 Weinheim, Germany

ISBN 978-1-11833929-9 (Cloth)
ISBN 978-1-11833930-5 (ePDF)
ISBN 978-1-11833931-2 (Mobi)
ISBN 978-1-11833932-9 (ePub)

Typeset in 11.5/14 point Bembo by MPS Limited, Chennai, India.
Printed in The United States of America.

10 9 8 7 6 5 4 3 2 1

To my wife, Jacinth,
who reviewed this manuscript more times than I did

Contents

Foreword

Students of investing look for a formula, a way of combining accounting and other information that will produce infallibly good investment results. Even Benjamin Graham, the founder and leading spirit of by far the most successful school of investment practice, spent a good deal of his time looking for such a formula. To this end, students read both technical works and the retrospective testimonies of high-performing investors. In both areas, they are largely disappointed.

The technical approaches have a meager record of success. A few notably good books have been written (for example Joel Greenblatt's *You Can be a Stock Market Genius* and *Graham and Dodd's Security Analysis*). But reported technical investment approaches rarely, if ever, lead to consistent, high-level returns (if they did they would be adopted by everyone and would become self-defeating).

Investment memoirs generally also disappoint students. They tend to be long on philosophy and short on advice for how to buy particular securities. However, as the works of successful investment practitioners, the memoirs do have much to recommend them. They describe, however non-specifically, investment approaches that worked in practice. And they capture an important aspect of investment success: that it depends more on character than on mathematical or technical ability. This is the consistent message of investment memoirs as a group.

The problem is that each memoir presents a unique perspective on the character traits necessary for investment success. Different authors emphasize different characteristics: patience, coolness in a crisis, wide-ranging curiosity, diligence in pursuit of information, independent thought, broad qualitative as opposed to detailed quantitative under-standing, humility, a proper appreciation of risk and uncertainty, a long time horizon, intellectual vigor and balance in analysis, a willingness to live outside the herd, and the ability to maintain a consistently critical perspective. Unfortunately, an investor with all these qualities is a rare bird indeed.

That is why Ronald Chan has done such a valuable service in writing this book. He has put together a set of thorough and rigorous portraits of a comprehensive range of notable value investors in a manageably short number of pages. His descriptions cover multiple generations from Walter Schloss and Irving Kahn to William Browne, multiple geographies from Asia to the United States to Europe and the full gamut of value investing styles. By combining descriptions of investment approaches with investor background, he illuminates the connection between individual character and effective investment practice. Taken as a whole, the book provides each practical value investor with the necessary material to sift through the historical records to find the style that is most appropriate to them.

Ronald Chan's work is an essential starting point for any nascent value investor and an invaluable reference for experienced investors.

BRUCE C. N. GREENWALD
Director, Heilbrunn Center for Graham and Dodd Investing
Robert Heilbrunn Professor of Finance and Asset Management

Preface

Try not to become a man of success but rather to become a man of value.

—Albert Einstein

The best advice I have ever received came from my father. When I began searching for a career after finishing college, he advised me to stay away from three potential headaches in business: labor, rent, and inventory.

As any labor-intensive business is likely to lead to office politics, my father advised that I look for a business that requires little manpower. Then, as the high office rents in a world city such as Hong Kong can easily squeeze profits, he said the ideal is to find a business that requires little office space. Finally, as handling any type of inventory requires both manpower and space, an inventory-based business should also be avoided.

Taking his advice to heart and looking for a business that met these three criteria, I found investment management to be a perfect fit. The labor force is my brain, the office need only accommodate a few desks, and the inventory is the investment positions recorded in brokerage accounts.

Although investment management may allow one to avoid the aforementioned headaches, becoming a successful investment manager still involves considerable challenges. It requires extensive knowledge of the financial markets and the ability to react to different market circumstances. It also requires a prudent strategy to achieve sustainable investment returns and a sensible investment philosophy to build the right investment model.

In developing my own investment philosophy, I read the work of Benjamin Graham, became aware of the phenomenal investment success of Warren Buffett, and came to realize that the value investing concept makes perfect sense. As Graham said, a value investment is "one which, upon thorough analysis, promises safety of principal and adequate return."

It is also difficult to argue with Buffett, who asked: "What is 'investing' if it is not the act of seeking value at least sufficient to justify the amount paid? Consciously paying more for a stock than its calculated value—in the hope that it can soon be sold for a still-higher price—should be labeled speculation."

After becoming a value investor myself, I began to explore the different types of investment valuation methods for sizing up businesses and investment opportunities. At first, I thought that the perfect valuation formula was the holy grail of investment success, but I soon came to realize that this is not the case. Instead, it is the right investment mindset, or temperament, that distinguishes the fair-to-good investor from the good-to-great one.

That realization prompted me to try to learn more about the mindsets and life stories of prominent value investors. However, all I could find were short profiles of these individuals and their investment track records, latest stock picks, and market predictions. Although the world recognizes their success, it seems that we are interested only in their views on the market outlook and their most recent investment performance, rather than who they really are, where they came from, and how they ended up becoming who they are today.

The thesis of this book, then, began to emerge. If I could hear the life stories, and understand the investment mindsets, of the world's most highly regarded value investors—and learn the details of their upbringing and career history—then perhaps I could begin to see what value means in their eyes. Is value, like beauty, in the eye of the beholder? Why do these individuals, despite age and cultural differences, share an investment philosophy?

Unlike other investment books, this book does not focus on a particular investment ratio or valuation methodology. Instead, it focuses on how life encounters and experiences directly and indirectly affect a person's investment mind-set and strategy.

To provide cultural diversity and demonstrate the international appeal of the value investing approach, the book features five value investors from North America, four from Asia, and three from Europe. Some have experience of different cultures. Mark Mobius of Templeton Emerging Markets Group, for example, was born in New York but has lived in Asia for more than 40 years. Frenchman Jean-Marie Eveillard moved to New York when he was in his late thirties and has lived there ever since. In many ways, the value mindset of these men has been shaped by their cultural experiences.

This book is not an in-depth analysis of the featured investors' track records. They have been in the industry long enough to win their peers' respect, whether due to their personalities and career experience or superior investment returns over the long term. What is of interest to me is how they got to where they are today.

For example, Irving Kahn is 106 years old and has been in the business for more than 84 years. Walter Schloss, who passed away recently at 95 years old, and had been described by Warren Buffett as the "super-investor from Graham-and-Doddsville," beat the market over 46 years.

Although the men featured in this book all have stellar investment records, they come from different walks of life and understand the notion of value differently.

Cheah Cheng Hye of Value Partners in Hong Kong, for example, worked as a journalist for 15 years before becoming a stock analyst and then a fund manager. Spaniard Francisco Paramés of Bestinver became a fund manager by accident in 1993 and has beaten the Spanish market ever since. His appreciation of value has been entirely self-taught.

Tokyo-based Shuhei Abe of the SPARX Group was once a bottom-up stock picker who could not imagine shorting a stock until he realized that Japan was going through a Depression, better known today as the country's "Lost Decade." To survive that decade, he improvised by creating a long-short fund based on the simple realization that if one knows what is underpriced, then one should also know what is over-priced. Abe and SPARX have thrived on the strategy ever since.

In sum, *The Value Investors: Lessons from the World's Top Fund Managers* shows that value investing is not a staid and old-fashioned investment strategy, but is dynamic and ever-evolving. Although the individuals featured in this book have different stories to tell, they exhibit similar personality traits. More important, they exhibit similar temperaments.

As Warren Buffett argued, "Success in investing doesn't correlate with I.Q. once you're above the level of 125. Once you have ordinary intelligence, what you need is the temperament to control the urges that get other people into trouble in investing."

RONALD W. CHAN
May 2012

CHAPTER 1

Free to Choose in Value Land

Walter Schloss
Walter & Edwin Schloss Associates

What does not destroy me, makes me stronger.

—*Friedrich Nietzsche*

*W*alter J. Schloss founded Walter J. Schloss and Associates in 1955. A student of Benjamin Graham, the father of value investing, Schloss had been finding undervalued securities in America since the 1930s. Having served as a securities analyst at the Graham-Newman Partnership in 1946, Schloss started his own fund when Graham decided to retire in 1955. Schloss's son Edwin joined the fund in the late 1960s, prompting an official name change in 1973 to Walter & Edwin Schloss Associates.

Charging no management fees but taking a 25 percent share of the profits, Schloss started off with $100,000 capital. At one point, the fund grew to roughly $350 million. From 1956 to 2002, it generated a 16 percent compound return annually (roughly 21 percent before profit sharing) versus the 10 percent per annum generated by the Standard & Poor's (S&P) 500.

Although a difference of 6 percent may not sound like much, the magic of compounding means that over this 46-year period, a $10,000 investment in the S&P 500 would have generated close to $900,000, whereas a Schloss investor would have made close to $11 million on the same investment.

A chartered financial analyst since 1963, Schloss was also the treasurer of Freedom House, a Washington, DC–based international nongovernmental organization that conducts research and advocacy on democracy, political freedom, and human rights.

Walter Schloss passed away on February 19, 2012, in Manhattan, New York. He was 95 years old.

3

Walter J. Schloss received his famous moniker, the "super-investor from Graham-and-Doddsville," not from any ordinary man but from the most admired and respected investing legend of all time—Warren Buffett—and it seems appropriate to allow the "sage of Omaha" to introduce him here.

Buffett singled Schloss out for praise in his 2006 letter to Berkshire Hathaway shareholders, noting that he had managed a "remarkably successful investment partnership" without taking "a single dime" unless his investors made money. Furthermore, he had done so without attending business school or even college, working "without a secretary, clerk or bookkeeper, his only associate being his son Edwin," an arts graduate, and generally flying in the face of prevailing business theories.

The letter continued: "When Walter and Edwin were asked in 1989 by *Outstanding Investors Digest*, 'How would you summarize your approach?' Edwin replied, 'We try to buy stocks cheap.' So much for Modern Portfolio Theory, technical analysis, macroeconomic thoughts and complex algorithms."

Buffett said that when he first publicly discussed Schloss's remarkable record in 1984, efficient market theory (EMT) held sway at most major business schools. According to EMT, as it was commonly taught at the time, Buffett noted, "No investor can be expected to overperform the stock market averages using only publicly-available information (though some will do so by luck). When I talked about Walter 23 years ago, his record forcefully contradicted this dogma."

Instead of taking the example of Schloss's obvious success on board, however, business school faculties went "merrily on their way presenting EMT as having the certainty of scripture," Buffett stated. "Typically, a finance instructor who had the nerve to question EMT had about as much chance of major promotion as Galileo had of being named Pope.

"Walter meanwhile went on over-performing, his job made easier by the misguided instructions that had been given to those young minds. After all, if you are in the shipping business, it's helpful to have all of your potential competitors be taught that the earth is flat."

Buffett concluded: "Maybe it was a good thing for his investors that Walter didn't go to college."

Living through the Great Depression

Walter Schloss was born in 1916 in New York City. He recalled: "When I was born, the world was at war, and there was a flu epidemic in the United States. My mother, Evelyn, was worried about catching the illness at the hospital, so she gave birth to me at home."

During the next two years, the flu pandemic that started in Europe (known as the Spanish flu) spread worldwide, killing more people than the total number killed in World War I. Fears of the disease prompted the Schloss family to move to Montclair, New Jersey, in 1918. However, "the place was too remote and inaccessible," Schloss said, "so after a while we moved back to New York City, and that's where I grew up."

From a young age, Schloss enjoyed traveling around the city by trolley car. He was so fascinated by the driver and his apparent privilege to travel freely wherever he liked that becoming a trolley car driver was his childhood dream job.

"Sometimes luck puts you in the right place at the right time! If I had been born a little earlier, I seriously would have considered becoming a trolley car driver. Luckily, trolley cars began to fade out and were replaced by buses in the 1930s and 40s, and so I ended up going to Wall Street," Schloss remarked.

Although still in middle school, Schloss was keenly aware of the 1929 stock market crash and the difficulties it unleashed. His mother lost her entire inheritance, and his father, Jerome, who had bought a U.S. company called Mathieson Alkali on margin, lost everything.

"My parents were honest people, but they had trouble financially because they were poor investors," Schloss said. "During the depression, my father learned his lesson and said to me, 'Anything terrible that doesn't happen to you is profit!' I took the advice to heart, so when I entered Wall Street, my goal was to not lose money!"

Turning 18 and finishing high school in 1934, Schloss decided to look for a job. With his mother's help, he found a job as a runner at brokerage house Carl M. Loeb & Co., which later changed its name to Loeb Rhoades, earning $15 per week.

"My father lost his job during the Depression, so I could not attend college and had to help my family," Schloss explained. "The economy was grim, and I remember seeing men on every street corner selling apples for a nickel apiece. Some family friends even criticized my mother for letting me work at a brokerage firm, as they believed there would be no more Wall Street by 1940. That was how pessimistic people were in those days."

As a runner, Schloss's duties included delivering paperwork and stock certificates to various brokerage houses for trade settlements each day. In effect, he was a messenger. Shortly after joining the company, he was promoted to the cashier's department—the "cage," as it was called—looking after and keeping track of stock certificate transfers between stockbrokers.

Schloss recollected, "After working for a year, I asked one of the partners, Mr. Armand Erpf, who was in charge of the statistical department, which is similar to the research department today, if I could become a securities analyst. He said that job wouldn't bring in any brokerage commissions, and so the answer was no.

"In those days, and perhaps it is true even to this day, bringing in business was the priority, and so business connections were more important than investment knowledge. Since a research analyst in those days would not advance very far within a company, who you knew was more important than what you knew."

Mr. Erpf did give young Schloss one very valuable piece of advice. He told him about a new book by Benjamin Graham and David Dodd called *Security Analysis*. "Read that book, and when you know everything in it, you won't have to read anything else," Schloss recalled him saying.

Reading the book gave Schloss the impetus to go to the New York Stock Exchange Institute to take finance and accounting courses. Completing these courses then made him eligible to take "Security Analysis," a course taught by the one and only Benjamin Graham. Paying roughly $15 per semester, he attended Graham's class from 1938 to 1940.

Learning directly from the father of value investing was a life-changing experience for Schloss: "Ben was simple, straightforward, and brilliant. Because he had a rough time during the Great Depression, his investment strategy was mainly to look for stocks that would provide downside protection, such as stocks selling below their working capital. The idea simply made a lot of sense to me, and I fell in love with his investment philosophy."

Schloss was particularly impressed by Graham's use of real-life examples to show which stocks were cheap and which were expensive: "He would also compare companies that came close to each other in alphabetical order. For example, he compared Coca-Cola to Colgate-Palmolive and statistically deduced that Colgate was cheaper.

"A lot of investment professionals took his class just to get investment tips, and they made money off his ideas, but Ben didn't mind because he was more into the academic exercise than making money. Unfortunately, I didn't profit from his ideas [at the time] because I had no money, but I learned a great deal."

The Meaning of Survival

World War II broke out in 1939, with the United States joining the war at the end of 1941 following the Japanese attack on Pearl Harbor. The patriotic 23-year-old Schloss decided to contribute to his country's war effort: "I remember it was the first Sunday of December when America was attacked. The next day, I went into the office and asked my boss whether I would still get my year-end bonus if I enlisted in the military. He said yes, and so I went straight to lower Manhattan to enlist. By Friday of that week, I had taken the oath of enlistment and was sent straight for training.

"I got on a big ship in New York, and we went zigzagging across the ocean so that submarines wouldn't sink us. We passed through Rio de Janeiro, then crossed the Atlantic Ocean to the Cape of Good Hope and the Indian Ocean to Bombay. Then, as the water was too shallow in the Persian Gulf, we had to switch to a British troopship named the HMT *Rohna* to get to Iran. I was lucky because if I had boarded that ship a few months later, I would have been on board when it was hit and sunk."

The Luftwaffe's sinking of the HMT *Rohna* in the Mediterranean in November 1943 constituted the single largest loss of U.S. troops at sea at one time.

Schloss served in the U.S. Army until 1945. He had been stationed in Iran, trained in code decryption, and was later assigned to the U.S. Signal Service Co., based at the Pentagon in Washington.

Having lived through roughly 18 economic recessions in his long life, Schloss felt that life is fragile, and when it comes to survival, money is of secondary importance in the grand scheme of things: "Life is tricky, and you really need to be lucky just to survive. When I joined the military, I really thought I'd never come home. My mother was so upset when I enlisted, but serving my country was my duty. This land has provided me with freedom and opportunities, and I am grateful for that!"

Schloss said that people frequently asked him how he survived the Great Depression and why he invested the way he did. "Obviously, Ben Graham was the teacher who showed me the way, but it was also my four years of military experience that shaped me into who I am. I learned that if I can simply survive in the market, just like surviving in the war, and not lose money, eventually I will make something.

"I also learned that life is short, so you need to be confident in yourself, and stick with what you like to do rather than do something you don't like but that will make you money!"

During his army years, Schloss often sent postcards to Benjamin Graham. One day, Graham sent him a letter explaining that his security analyst was leaving the company and asked whether Schloss would consider replacing him. It was too good an opportunity to pass up, and shortly after the war ended Schloss went to work for Graham, taking up his new position on January 2, 1946, for a salary of $50 a week.

Net-Nets

Schloss and Graham had very similar investment mindsets. Schloss's priorities were not to lose money and to survive in the market, whereas Graham's were to seek downside protection and to diversify his investment portfolio to minimize individual stock risks. Working for Graham from 1946 to 1955, Schloss's duty was to find stocks that were selling below their working capital—"net-nets." The idea behind a net-net is to value a company based on its current net assets by taking cash and cash equivalents at full value, then giving a discount to accounts receivable and inventory, and finally deducting all of the company's liabilities. The net-net value is then derived by dividing the resulting sum by the total shares outstanding.

Because financial information was not easily accessible in the old days and investor sentiment was generally poor after the Great

Depression, many stocks traded well below their net-net value. Buying these stocks was similar to paying 50 cents for a dollar.

Schloss elaborated: "There were many net-net stocks in the 1930s and 1940s. Our idea was to find stocks that were trading at two-thirds of working capital because when they eventually matched their working capital per share, then we would have made 50 percent on our investment. In the 1950s, these stocks were harder to find, and so we had to work even harder."

He further explained that the main issues with this strategy were that franchise value and management quality were generally ignored. "So, in most cases, we found secondary companies that did not appeal to the general public in the first place. Besides, many of them had big book values, but not necessarily good earnings, and so they were sometimes in trouble. To reduce risk, Ben really stressed the importance of diversification. The good thing, however, was that they were cheap enough and provided a good margin of safety. Thus, our contrarian approach worked."

In the process of identifying net-nets, Schloss met the future sage of Omaha, then in his early twenties, at the annual meeting of wholesaler Marshall-Wells.

Schloss recalled, "Warren was at the annual meeting because he also spotted an opportunity. He later came to work for Ben in 1954, and we shared the same room and worked on the liquidation values of companies together. Warren has a good sense of humor and is an honest gentleman."

As for the young Buffett, Schloss had always been "Big Walter," clearly a kind of brother figure with whom he enjoyed sharing ideas.

Today, Buffett's Berkshire Hathaway owns auto insurance firm GEICO (Government Employees Insurance Company), but 50 percent of the company was once owned by Graham-Newman. According to Schloss, GEICO turned down Graham's initial bid in 1948, but his subsequent bid of $750,000 got him the 50 percent share.

Schloss explained: "I happened to be sitting next to Ben when the lawyer called to confirm the deal. Because it represented almost a quarter of Graham-Newman's capital, Ben knew only that he was buying the business at a cheap price; he had no idea of its growth potential. He turned to me and said, 'Walter, if this deal doesn't work out, we can always liquidate it and get our money back!' That was the type of downside protection Ben was looking for."

After closing the deal, Graham discovered that an investment company was not permitted to hold such a high stake in an insurance company without regulatory approval. To settle the resulting conflict, he was forced to turn GEICO into a public company and distribute its shares among Graham-Newman's investors at cost.

Although Schloss received a number of GEICO shares, he later sold them to pay for the births of his son, Edwin, and daughter, Stephanie: "I didn't benefit financially from the GEICO deal, but I ended up with a son and a daughter. Not a bad deal!"

In 1955, Graham decided to retire and move to California. Schloss, feeling confident in his ability to run money after having worked for his mentor for nine and a half years, thought immediately of starting his own fund, but did not initially have the nerve to tell Graham because of his great respect for the man. Given a push by clients and friends, including Buffett, Schloss finally decided to set up on his own fund. After raising money from 19 investors, he founded Walter J. Schloss and Associates in 1955.

Benjamin Graham, who passed away in 1976, was ultimately much more to Schloss than mentor and colleague. He was the person who showed the young man the way to financial freedom and how to accumulate wealth safely and securely over time. One wonders to this day whether, had he not read Graham's *Security Analysis*, Schloss would indeed have pursued his early dream of becoming a trolley car driver.

Recalling Graham in a piece titled "Benjamin Graham and Security Analysis: A Reminiscence," Schloss wrote:

Ben Graham was an original thinker as well as a clear thinker. He had high ethical standards and was modest and unassuming. He was one of a kind . . . He tried to keep things simple. He wrote that he didn't believe security analysts should use more than arithmetic and possibly a little algebra for any investment decision.

In re-reading the preface to the first edition of *Security Analysis*, I am impressed all over again with Ben's views: "[We] are concerned chiefly with concepts, methods, standards, principles, and above all with logical reasoning. We have stressed theory not for itself alone but for its value in practice. We have tried to avoid prescribing standards which are too stringent to follow or technical methods which are more trouble than they are worth."

Ben had been hurt by the Depression, so he wanted to invest in things that would protect him on the downside. The best way to do this was to lay out rules which, if followed, would reduce his chance of loss . . . The ability to think clearly in the investment field without the emotions that are attached to it is not an easy undertaking. Fear and greed tend to affect one's judgment. Because Ben was not really very aggressive about making money, he was less affected by these emotions than were many others.

Of all the things that Ben accomplished in his lifetime, *Security Analysis* was, to me, his greatest achievement . . . It was a privilege to know him.[1]

Setting the Right Pace

For Schloss, going solo really meant going solo. He had no secretary or research assistant, and as he required only a desk and a filing cabinet, he subleased a closet-size space at Tweedy, Brown & Co., a stock brokerage firm he regularly dealt with while working at Graham-Newman.

Being naturally thrifty, it was not difficult for Schloss to keep expenses down as he began hunting for bargains. Eschewing the grueling hours of today's investment professional, he worked from 9:00 A.M. to 4:30 P.M. with no ticker tape to track stocks. Instead, his main source of stock quotes was the daily newspaper.

Rather than employ a variety of methods to search for investment ideas, he mainly looked for stocks that were trading at new lows. Then he would check the financial statistics and performance of the companies in question through Value Line, an independent investment research provider. If a company suited him, he would request its financial reports

---

[1] This article appears in Schloss's private writings from 1976.

and proxy statements to further investigate the soundness of the opportunity.

Schloss explained, "I used the same investment approach I used at Graham-Newman—finding net-net stocks. It was all about capital preservation because I had to serve in the best interests of my investors. Many of them were not wealthy, and they needed me to generate returns that would allow them to cover their living expenses.

"Because I don't like stress and prefer to avoid it, I never focus too much on market news and economic data. They always worry investors! Besides, I am not good at market timing, so when people ask me what I think the market is doing, their guess is as good as mine." Instead, he said, he concentrated primarily on the price of a stock and its value, an exercise he has greater confidence in.

When Schloss started his own fund, he established the rule that he would never disclose its investment holdings: "I did that for several reasons. First, I found that investors like to focus on losing stocks, and I'd become really stressed if they came crying and asking me about what had happened. Second, I found that if people knew what I was buying, then I'd get more competition."

He employed an example from his Graham-Newman days to illustrate. After he came across a cheap stock called Lukens Steel, the firm bought some shares and expected to buy more. Then, Schloss recalled, "One day Ben Graham had lunch with a man who kept asking him what he liked. Not wanting to be rude, Ben said he liked Lukens Steel. I don't know whether that man bought a great amount, but the stock went above our buying range shortly afterward."

Refusing to disclose his investment holdings had another benefit: It put Schloss at ease because he admitted that he was always too early getting into a stock position: "If a stock is cheap, I start buying. I never put a stop loss on my holdings because if I like a stock in the first place, I like it more if it goes down. Somehow I find it difficult to buy a stock that has gone up."

Schloss explained that because his strategy had always been to look for the margin of safety between a stock's worth and its trading price, the larger this margin was, the happier he was. Having said that, it often took patience to wait for a cheap stock to gradually reflect its true worth over time.

"My average holding period was about four to five years," Schloss explained, "and so there was plenty of time for cheap stocks to get back to their true worth. Besides, they would be treated as long-term capital gains for tax purposes." He fondly recalled Ben Graham once saying that "one should buy stocks the way you buy groceries and not the way you buy perfume," noting that "I felt that I was a grocery store owner, holding stocks as my inventory. Sometimes these stocks paid dividends, and so they were worth the wait. Eventually, someone would come along and offer a good price for my inventory, and I would sell."

Unlike many fund managers who like to talk to management and understand a company's business, Schloss's sole interest was in looking at the statistical side of a stock. Doing so meant "focusing on the downside and not losing money," he explained. "When a stock trades below its working capital, the investor begins to get protection."

Schloss elaborated: "I always like to find companies with no to low debt because debt complicates things. I also like to see whether management owns enough of the company's stock to serve in its best interests. But you often have to keep track of management's actions, digging into the footnotes of financial statements to see if they are honest people.

"When I buy a stock, I never visit or talk to management because I think that a company's financial figures are good enough to tell the story. Besides, management always says something good about the company, which may affect my judgment. I know a lot of good investors who like to talk to management and visit companies, but that's not me. I don't like that kind of stress, and if I had had to run around visiting so many companies, I would have been dead after a few years!"

What is ultimately important, Schloss said, is to be comfortable with who you are and to make sure you can sleep at night because managing other people's money is a heavy responsibility.

The exercise that he always found most difficult and challenging was selling a stock: "Since I focus so much on the downside risk, the problem is that I don't emphasize the growth potential of a company and its profit too much. When it reaches a reasonable price, I sell."

Schloss recalled his experience with a cement company called South-down to illustrate the possible disadvantage of his approach: "I bought a lot of it at $12 or something similar. After two or three years, when it reached about $28, I sold it because it had reached my calculated value, and I didn't focus too much on its growth opportunities. It reached $70 a while later. I could only be humble and move on to find the next cheap stock.

"Sometimes in life you cannot regret things that didn't work out or things that could have worked out better. The challenge in life is knowing what's next. Like my father taught me, 'Nothing terrible happening to you is profit!' After all, my goal was to keep losses down, and if I could catch a few stocks going up, compound returns would work their magic."

In the late 1960s, Edwin Schloss decided to join his father in the business, and from then on the two worked as a team to search for undervalued stocks. In 1973, the company changed its name to Walter & Edwin Schloss Associates to reflect the partnership. To keep expenses down, the father and son hired no additional employees.

Over the years, the Schlosses remained focused on finding net-net stocks, but the world changed and these stocks became almost impossible to find. A strategy adjustment based on book value was in order.

Schloss explained: "We changed our strategy a little, but remained true to Graham's principle of downside protection. We looked for stocks that were selling below their book value. What we tried to do was to buy assets at a discount instead of buying earnings. Earnings can change quickly, but assets don't, and so the new strategy worked well for a while."

However, it was not long before even this new book value strategy and Graham's way of investing simply became inapplicable in the modern world. For Schloss, it was difficult to judge whether the world had become smarter or riskier. Either way, retirement beckoned, and Schloss decided to close down the business in 2001 after more than 45 years of managing money.

He explained: "I had turned 85, and one day my son said to me, 'Dad, I can't find cheap stocks anymore!' So I said, 'Let's go out of business!' We liquidated the partnership and gave back the money to investors." One thing Schloss learned in his long life was the importance of avoiding stress: "Finding cheap stocks became too stressful, and so it was time to stop looking."

Know Thyself

"When it comes to investing," Schloss advised, "my suggestion is to first understand your strengths and weaknesses, and then devise a simple strategy so that you can sleep at night! Remember that a share of stock represents a part of a business, and so you need to understand its financials before making a judgment. When you have made a sound decision, make sure you have the courage to stay true to your convictions and not let the market affect your emotions. After all, investing should be fun and challenging, not stressful and worrying."

Every value investor is different. Although most probably adhere to the principles Benjamin Graham put forward in *Security Analysis* and *The Intelligent Investor*, Schloss stressed the importance of knowing oneself.

For example, Warren Buffett believes in portfolio concentration, but Schloss's own personality was more suited to diversification: "I always held 50 to 100 stocks at any given time because it would have been very stressful if one particular stock had turned against me. Psychologically, I am just built differently than Warren. I see that there are many people trying to be like Warren, but they should take note that he is not only a good analyst; he is also a good judge of people and businesses. I know my limitations, so I'd rather invest in the way I am most comfortable with."

Benjamin Graham inspired a group of highly successful "super-investors." Obviously, as Buffett has pointed out, these individuals were not just lucky; they had also acquired a similar skill set and the mentality to beat the market year after year.

Schloss attempted to explain the making of these super-investors: "I think investing is an art, and we tried to be as logical and unemotional as possible. Because we understood that investors are usually affected by the market, we could take advantage of the market by being rational. As Graham said, 'The market is there to serve you, not to guide you!'"

Speaking of the Graham–inspired group of super-investors as a whole, he said: "I think, in the first place, that we are honest people. We have tried to prevent our investors from losing money, and we have not tried to make money at their expense. I don't know about the others, but I am 95 years old now, and I sometimes forget what I am supposed to remember. One thing I will always remember, though, is how

America has given me the opportunity to invest and the freedom to do what I enjoy doing. Being grateful for that opportunity, my goal was never just to bring value to my investors, but also to do what's right for those who trusted me!"

Again, no one sums up Walter J. Schloss as perfectly as Warren Buffett, and so, just as he began this chapter, he will also have the final word. In "The Superinvestors of Graham-and-Doddsville," an influential article that Buffett published in the fall 1984 issue of *Hermes*, the magazine of the Columbia Business School, he wrote:

> He [Walter] never forgets that he is handling other people's money and this reinforces his normal strong aversion to loss. He has total integrity and a realistic picture of himself. Money is real to him and stocks are real—and from this flows an attraction to the 'margin of safety' principle.
>
> Walter has diversified enormously. . . . He knows how to identify securities that sell at considerably less than their value to a private owner. *And that's all he does.* He doesn't worry about whether it's January, he doesn't worry about whether it's Monday, he doesn't worry about whether it's an election year. He simply says, if a business is worth a dollar and I can buy it for 40 cents, something good may happen to me. And he does it over and over and over again. He owns many more stocks than I do and is far less interested in the underlying nature of the business; I don't seem to have very much influence on Walter. That's one of his strengths; no one has much influence on him.[2]

---

[2] Copyright 1984. Hermes, Columbia Business School. Reprinted with permission.

CHAPTER 2

Once Upon a Time on Wall Street

Irving Kahn
Kahn Brothers Group

The world is a tragedy to those who feel, but a comedy to those who think.

—*Horace Walpole*

*I*rving Kahn is the chairman of Kahn Brothers Group, an investment management and advisory firm that he founded in 1978 with his two sons, Alan and Thomas.

One of the early attendees of Benjamin Graham's class on security analysis in the late 1920s, Kahn became Graham's teaching assistant in 1931. He then worked closely with Graham over the next 25 years until the great teacher decided to retire in 1956.

Kahn is a founding member of the New York Society of Security Analysts (NYSSA) in 1937 and the Financial Analysts Journal in 1945. He also became a chartered financial analyst (CFA) in 1963, when he was among the first group of applicants to take the CFA exam administered by the Institute of Chartered Financial Analysts, the predecessor of today's CFA Institute. He has served as a director of Grand Union Stores, Kings County Lighting, West Chemical, and Wilcox & Gibbs.

At the time of writing in late 2011, Kahn was 106 years old. Currently the oldest active money manager on Wall Street, he is undoubtedly among the earliest practitioners of security analysis, if not one of the first value investors of the twentieth century.

"When the Dow Jones Industrial Average dropped 85 percent—from 350 to 50 points between 1929 and 1933—the Great Depression became very real to me," Irving Kahn recalled. "When my boss reduced my salary from $100 to $60, he asked me why was I smiling, and I said, 'I thought you were going to fire me!'"

There is an old saying that goes: "A recession is when your neighbor loses his job. A depression is when you lose yours." Certainly, life was hard in the 1930s, but Kahn always had an optimistic attitude and kept himself busy. His motto: "There is always something to do. You just need to look harder, be creative, and be a little flexible!"

Born in 1905 in New York, Kahn grew up in a working-class household headed by parents who had emigrated from Poland and Russia. He said, "My mother, Esther, and my father, Saul, were willing to drop the language, religion, and friends of their own countries and come to America to look for a new life. My respect for their courage and determination prompted me to study very hard from a young age because I wanted to find a well-paid job one day to support them."

After graduating from DeWitt Clinton High School, Kahn went to the City College of New York to study liberal arts. However, he dropped out after two years and went to Wall Street in 1928: "Like most kids, I wanted to get a well-paid job, but I didn't know where to find one. At that time the stock market was hot, and there were a lot of advertisements and public relations items in the newspapers about Wall Street, so I walked into a Wall Street firm, Hammerschlag, Borg, and asked if they were looking for a boy. They gave me a job right away."

Kahn noted that his generation flourished in the 1920s because the influx of immigrants from Western and Eastern Europe helped to fuel the economy. With no real threats from labor unions or exclusive trades, jobs were abundant and the American Dream was widely achievable. Indeed, the U.S. unemployment rate was less than 5 percent in 1929, although dreams began to vanish after the stock market crash in October of that year. By 1933, the unemployment rate had risen as high as 25 percent.

"My first job was at 11 Wall Street, which is the New York Stock Exchange building. After one week of working there, I decided to quit because I thought the people were crazy. They were running around and screaming at each other during trading hours, and they were like clowns! I felt that I wasn't learning anything, and so I went to my boss.

He convinced me not to quit, and he sent me to the main office where I became a broker's assistant, doing securities research," Kahn explained.

Kahn admitted that he initially knew nothing about the duties his job entailed. To learn more about what it meant to be an analyst, he went to the public library each day to study the finance market and its history. His own study of the boom-and-bust cycle of the U.S. economy led him to begin questioning the stock market euphoria that prevailed on Wall Street.

His bearish outlook further developed after he read about the early-1920s Florida real estate boom in which house prices easily doubled in a matter of weeks, and speculators were leveraging heavily by putting down just 10 percent of the property price in cash. In 1925, the sky-rocketing real estate prices began to stall, as fools became more difficult to find. Then, in 1926, prices finally collapsed completely when Mother Nature unleashed two severe hurricanes that virtually destroyed the state. Many developers and speculators went bust.

Although the Florida debacle gave Americans their first taste of the Great Depression, the search for easy money continued. In 1927, hot money began to pour into the stock market, turning Wall Street into a virtual casino. Similar to the case of the Florida real estate boom, excessive leverage was common, as it was easy to buy a stock on a 10 percent margin. Kahn believed a collapse was simply a matter of time.

Kahn explained, "The real estate bust in Florida showed me that any market mania comes up against hard reality in the end. Since stock prices were trading at extremely high levels in 1929, I really couldn't assign a number to what companies were worth, and so I thought of shorting the market.

"From some of the financial history books I read that discussed the market cycle, I learned that stocks in certain industries were especially volatile, and copper was one. I looked at the stock index list, and decided to short a copper company called Magma Copper. Because I had little money, I had to ask my brother-in-law, who was a lawyer, to open a brokerage account for me.

"With $50, I shorted the stock in the summer, and my brother-in-law said it wouldn't be long before I lost all my money because the market was going up, and I was telling it to go down. In October 1929, when the stock market crashed, my $50 became nearly $100. That was the first trade of my life."

Despite this good start in the stock market, Kahn found it difficult to live through the Great Depression. One of the moments of greatest uncertainty for him, and probably for any American alive at the time, was President Franklin D. Roosevelt's decision to impose a bank holiday from March 5 to 12, 1933, closing every bank in the country for eight days.

Kahn told the story: "It was a shocking moment for me because after eight days, many banks would never be able to reopen their doors. I remember the whole trouble began months earlier when many people initiated a run on the banks. When President Roosevelt took office, he announced a nationwide bank holiday to shut down the banking system. In the next eight days, he passed the Emergency Banking Act to restore confidence by guaranteeing deposits 100 percent. The deal was well received, and so when the stock market reopened on March 15, it went up 15 percent. Those eight days of uncertainty as a nation were the gloomiest of my career!"

Looking back, Kahn joked, "The Depression taught me what frugality means and the importance of not losing money. Because I was so frugal, I walked home to my apartment in lower Manhattan for lunch so that I could save on expenses. My kids must have thought they had a wealthy father because I could always come home in the middle of the day. But obviously, I wasn't rich."

Humility aside, Kahn actually did quite well during the Depression years. By 1939, he had made enough money to move out of public housing into a house in the suburbs, moving to Belle Harbor in Queens. Contributing to his success was the opportunity to learn from and work closely with one of the most sensible investors of the time: Benjamin Graham.

Becoming Graham's Disciple

While working at Hammerschlag, Borg in 1928, Kahn shared his market concerns with his colleagues, and the head bookkeeper recommended that he seek out Benjamin Graham at the Cotton Exchange on Beaver Street to gain greater insight. After meeting the man and learning that he would soon begin teaching a class on security analysis at Columbia University, Kahn enrolled without hesitation.

He recalled: "It was a two-hour course one evening a week. Ben used real examples of both popular and unpopular securities to illustrate the application of security analysis. Many students took his class year after year because they got many stock ideas from him and profited from them. Ben didn't care if students made money from his ideas because he was more into analysis as an intellectual exercise than for the financial reward.

"Before the crash in 1929, a student asked Ben if he should buy the warrants of utility company American and Foreign Power Co.—the Internet stock of the day. Ben asked the student to calculate the total market value of outstanding warrants, which turned out to be much larger than the market value of Pennsylvania Railroad, a blue chip company. This exercise showed the whole class how distorted the market had become, and, of course, Ben was right because American and Foreign Power soon tumbled following the crash."

Reminiscing about Graham's lectures, Kahn said that the great teacher encouraged every student to participate and engage with the investment topics they discussed. Using up-to-date examples, Graham illustrated the merits of security analysis.

Kahn explained in greater detail: "Ben always believed in the Socratic approach. He never provided students with a ready answer, believing that through thorough discussions and rational deductions, solid conclusions would be reached. I remember asking him about the word 'tranche' as it applied to finance. Instead of providing the definition right away, Ben asked me to look it up in the dictionary. I discovered that it means 'slice' in French. Ben believed that if he told me the answer right away, I would forget it, but if I took the initiative to look it up myself, then I would always remember it."

Kahn met his future wife, Ruth, in Graham's class. The two were married from 1931 until 1996, when Ruth passed away. They had three sons, the third of whom they named Thomas Graham Kahn in honor of their teacher.

In addition to getting married in 1931, Kahn also found himself a new side career as a teacher. Graham's assistant, Leo Stern, decided to step down that year, and Kahn was quickly asked to fill the spot: "I had the honor of working for Ben until 1956, when he retired. Not only did I come to truly understand the essence of security analysis by serving as his teaching assistant, but I was also able to earn some extra money. My duties were to prepare statistical analyses for class discussions and to mark case studies and exams."

Over the next 25 years, Kahn was privileged to share insights not only with Graham, but also with many other future investing legends, including William Ruane, Walter Schloss, Charles Brandes, and Warren Buffett.

"Class began at 4:00 P.M., which was an hour after market close in those days. Ben and I would take the subway together from Wall Street to Columbia University, and we would talk about everything. Soon Ben became not just a mentor, but also a dear friend. We would go on skiing trips together. I remember in the days before ski lifts Ben told me to put snakeskin on the bottom of my skis to make it easier to climb up the snow. Those trips provide fond memories of Ben," Kahn recalled.

Kahn was a true confidant of Graham's, and many of the statistical and comparative analyses he prepared were used as examples in Graham and David Dodd's influential *Security Analysis*, published in 1934. This seminal work transformed the world of finance by introducing investors to fundamental analysis. It also garnered Graham the moniker "father of value investing" or "father of security analysis."

Seeing the world through Graham's eyes also helped Kahn to compile statistical materials for Graham's *Storage and Stability* in 1937. Graham's recognition of the hardships caused by price deflation during the Great Depression, which devastated the lives of farmers and workers, led to his proposal to regulate the supply and demand of important raw materials and commodities in the hope of creating a reserve basket of commodities to achieve price stability and restore economic growth. Although the book was not widely read by the general populace, it was well received by politicians and economists, including John Maynard Keynes.

After Benjamin Graham officially retired in 1956, and until his death at age 82 on September 21, 1976, he lived in California and France. Kahn later worked with Robert Milne to write a monograph of the great man for the Financial Analysts Research Foundation. In the piece, titled "Benjamin Graham: The Father of Financial Analysis," he wrote about several remarkable aspects of the investment legend:

He had several extraordinary characteristics. His speed of thought was so great that most people were puzzled at how he could resolve a complicated question directly after having heard it. His mental training came from his rigorous study of mathematics, particularly geometry, which required close and exact reasoning before accepting or rejecting either a premise or a conclusion.

He had another extraordinary characteristic in the breadth and depth of his memory. This explains why he could read Greek, Latin, Spanish, and German. Even more remarkable, without having studied Spanish formally, he was able to translate a Spanish novel into literary English so professionally that it was accepted by an American publisher.

In his early years, Ben was both a skier and a tennis player. But his real pleasure was to exercise his mind over a wide range of subjects far beyond his specialties in the world of finance. He loved music, especially the major operas, for the wisdom of their lyrics, as well as their melodies. He had a private, but serious hobby of making improvements in the field of plane geometry. He actually patented several versions of a simplified protractor and a circular slide rule.

In sum, Ben Graham was such a rare combination of qualities [that] only those who knew him well over the years can do full justice to presenting the whole man. In the world of finance Ben's epitaph will be as was Christopher Wren's in St. Paul's, "If you seek his monument—look about you.

Preaching Value

In addition to being closely associated with Benjamin Graham, Kahn has had an extremely successful investment career in his own right. After working at Hammerschlag, Borg for a few years, he joined Loeb, Rhoades & Co. as a securities analyst. Then, around 1940, he joined Wertheim & Co.

He recalled, "The Great Depression was like a big storm that sank every ship. It was easy to make money if you had the right approach and knew where to look because some companies were in good shape and had nothing but cash. For example, some export companies were not severely affected by the Depression, but they were beaten down and had net cash per share that was much greater than their stock price. You didn't have to be very smart to find value. All you needed was the right investment model."

At Wertheim & Co., Kahn specialized in the mining industry. His reputation as Graham's disciple and a strong advocate of fundamental analysis garnered introductions to many successful businessmen and wealthy clients. Recommending undervalued stocks to these individuals also earned him healthy commissions. Kahn's growing salary not only allowed him to begin managing his own wealth, but also afforded him an opportunity to invest in the Graham-Newman Corporation, the investment firm run by Benjamin Graham.

In the 1950s, Kahn was made a partner at J.R. Williston Co. Although he remained with the company for only a few years, he developed a good working relationship with his assistant, William "Bill" DeLuca, who is now in his late eighties and works closely with Kahn to this day.

In the early 1960s, Kahn joined Abraham & Company as partner. He stayed with the firm until 1978, when he and his two sons decided to form Kahn Brothers & Co. He explained: "In 1975, Lehman Brothers acquired Abraham & Co. The firm became too big, and I didn't really enjoy the environment. Since my two sons, Alan and Thomas, and my colleague, Bill, were also working at the firm and felt the same way, we decided to start something of our own."

A rather noteworthy event is that shortly after starting up Kahn Brothers, Kahn decided to buy a seat on the New York Stock Exchange to facilitate stock trades. Paying around $100,000 in 1978, the seat was worth approximately $3 million in 2005. When the Exchange went public, Kahn received $500,000 in cash and 77,000 shares of the newly listed company.

Discussing the investment strategy he has applied throughout his career, Kahn said: "Net-net stocks were easy to find in the early days. All I had to do was to look over annual reports and study balance sheets. I tried to find companies that had dependable assets such as cash, land, and real properties. Then, I made sure they didn't have too much debt and had decent prospects. If these stocks traded at below their net working capital, then I would be interested in buying them.

"I understand that net-net stocks are not too common anymore, but today's investors should not complain too much because there were only a handful of industries in which to look for stocks in the old days. Now there are so many different types of businesses in so many different countries that investors can easily find something. Besides, the Internet has made more information available. If you complain that you cannot find opportunities, then that means you either haven't looked hard enough or you haven't read broadly enough!"

A voracious reader, Kahn devours everything except fiction, which adds little value to his search for investment ideas. In addition to reading several newspapers a day, he also reads scientific journals and technology magazines regularly. A close follower of the latest news and trends, he has read thousands of nonfiction books—most of which are heavily marked with his apt comments.

When asked how he has generated investment ideas for so many years, he responds that it is really all about absorbing numerous types of information, from economic news to science, from psychology to annual reports, and from financial journals to history, and then combining them to generate a broad perspective on the future.

He further explained, "Reading about science gives me an open mind! When European scientists discovered uranium and found that it could produce power, people thought they had had too much to drink. Many scientific ideas that sounded unbelievable in the early days of my life have now become reality, so it is important to read science books and to learn about the future."

When hot ideas fall into his value territory during economic recessions and market corrections, Kahn buys. "Real investors should never feel bearish because the time to buy value is when markets go down!"

One of the high-tech businesses that captured Kahn's interest in the past 15 years was water purification equipment maker Osmonics. He noticed early on that the world's growing population would require cleaner water, and so, when the company's stock fell tremendously after the technology bubble burst, he bought it without hesitation. General Electric acquired the company in 2003, and Kahn generated a nice profit from his investment.

Around the same time that he became interested in Osmonics, Kahn also began to realize that the world's growing population would need more food and that the genetically modified seeds produced by Monsanto would help to increase the food supply. Environmentalists were more skeptical, however, and their attacks on the company pushed the stock price down to around $20. Trusting his own research, Kahn bought the stock as it represented good value. In just a couple of years, it was trading at well above $60.

In addition to the value of reading about a wide range of subjects, Kahn believes that successful investing requires patience, discipline, and skepticism. As undervalued investments are not usually recognized by the broader market in the beginning, patience is required to see how they play out over time.

Discipline is crucial because allowing others to suggest what stocks are worth breeds lazy thinking. The wise investor must be disciplined enough to do the hard work necessary and to look into the numbers before making any investment decisions. In this respect, discipline breeds independent thinking.

Finally, a little skepticism also comes in handy because although cheap stocks are revealed by their financial figures, these numbers are reported by companies' management. Thus, a bit of caution is always warranted, as investors must look beyond the numbers to get a sense of the quality of the corporate executives involved.

"In the early days, many companies had opaque financial reporting standards," Kahn recalled, "and so it took quite some effort to read between the lines and delve into the footnotes of financial statements to find out about the quality of a company's management. Sometimes the lack of information made things difficult, and sometimes company executives did not treat shareholders as if they were business owners."

To improve the quality of security analysis by coordinating with corporate executives, Kahn, along with Benjamin Graham and 18 other security analysts, founded the New York Society of Security Analysts in 1937. The organization started out as a small group of security analysts who got together during their lunch hour to discuss stocks and investing in general. As these gatherings turned into regular meetings, the NYSSA was conceived.

According to the NYSSA's mission statement, the organization's purpose is "to establish and maintain a high standard of professional ethics in the security analysis field, and to promote proper understanding of the function of financial and security analysis and the operation of the security markets." Starting life with fewer than two dozen members, the NYSSA is today the CFA Institute's largest member society, boasting more than 10,000 members.

Kahn commented, "We tried to arrange meetings with corporate executives, and we convinced them to come to a cheap restaurant in New York City, where we showed them the advantage of speaking to us because we could help promote their companies if we could learn more about their businesses. Those meetings were very useful at first, but over the years they have turned into what we call 'analysts' conference calls,' which are less productive because what executives try to do now is to manage analysts' expectations."

Always preaching the value of security analysis, Kahn also became a founding member of the *Financial Analysts Journal* in 1945. In honor of its sixtieth anniversary in 2005, he contributed an article, titled "Early Days at the *Financial Analysts Journal*," which discussed the publication's essence. He wrote: "The approach we pursued was to give how-to advice for day-to-day practice on analyzing company, industry, and national statistics and facts. Others, particularly the academic authors that became attracted to the *Journal*, pursued the theoretical side . . . the challenge was then and continues today: how to bridge the gap between theory and practice."

Backtracking to 1977, Kahn contributed another article, titled "Lemmings Always Lose" to the journal, in which he outlined the simple rules of intelligent investing:

1. Don't depend on recent or current figures to forecast futures prices; remember that many others knew them before you did.
2. Prices are continuously molded by fears, hopes, and unreliable estimates; capital is always at risk unless you buy better than average values.
3. Remember that many complex factors—such as accounting choices and the human problems within management and with large shareholders—lie behind reported earnings.
4. Disregard the competition at your peril—they are always attacking your company's trade position and its earnings.
5. Don't trust quarterly earnings. Verify reports through the source and application statement. Figures can lie and liars can figure.

The analyst must both practice, and to his client preach, patience. Fortunately for us analysts, it is unlikely that in this ever-changing world any formula will ever successfully replace the study and objective analysis of individual securities.

A Centenarian Diet

Kahn believes that Wall Street has always been a poor judge of value. First, it never learns from the past, often repeating the same investment mistakes. The 1929 crash, the Nifty-Fifty of the early 1970s, October 1987, the fall of Long-Term Capital Management, the dot-com bubble, and even the Lehman crisis all have similar plots, albeit different characters and investment products. As the saying goes, "History doesn't repeat itself, but it does rhyme." Kahn added, "If the world had more value investors, we would never get into any of these messes!"

Second, people on Wall Street often put so much effort into making money that they lead stressful, unhealthy lifestyles. Kahn questions the value of a life with wealth but without health.

A centenarian who has now been in the investment business for more than 80 years, Kahn has learned a bit about how to stay both healthy and wealthy: "Don't drink or smoke. Get yourself a nutritious diet. Stay in motion. Meet people from around the world and be inspired. Read a lot, and read about the things that are not possible now, but will be in the future. As long as you keep your mind sharp and busy, you will see good things happen!"

Participants in the Longevity Genes Project undertaken by the Albert Einstein College of Medicine at Yeshiva University in New York City, Kahn and his siblings are living testimony that longevity may be genetic. His two sisters, Helen and Lee, died in 2011 and 2005 at nearly 110 and 102 years old, respectively. His "baby brother" Peter is now 101.

The college's researchers have hypothesized that the Kahns' extremely high levels of "good" high-density lipoprotein cholesterol have created protective effects to fend off age-related infirmities. Kahn is eagerly awaiting their discovery of whether this is indeed true.

Genes aside, researchers have also found that centenarians are generally extroverts and friendly people with a stable social network. They tend to have an open mind and focus on the bright side of life. They rarely whine about life's difficulties despite having lived through poverty and fear during the Great Depression and World War II. In effect, these people avoid stress and are masters of letting go.

Kahn remarked, "People are always worried about the economy and the world, especially since the financial crisis of 2008 and Europe's sovereign debt crisis in 2011. I feel that people should learn to be optimistic because life goes on, and sometimes favorable surprises come out of the blue, whether due to new policies or scientific breakthroughs.

"That said, the world is full of complications, and the media are full of advertising. Stop buying things that you don't need, and start focusing on the essentials; then you will live long and be happy. In life, the goal is to achieve happiness, so start thinking about the things that count!"

Commenting on his fame within investment circles, Kahn joked, "You get to be famous when you live long enough!"

CHAPTER 3

The Making of a Contrarian

Thomas Kahn
Kahn Brothers Group

Worldly wisdom teaches that it is better for reputation to fail
conventionally than to succeed unconventionally.
                                              —*John Maynard Keynes*

*T*homas Graham Kahn is president of Kahn Brothers Group, Inc.
Through its two subsidiaries, Kahn Brothers Advisors LLC and
Kahn Brothers LLC, the company provides investment management
and advisory services and broker-dealer services.

*Irving Kahn and his sons, Alan and Thomas, founded Kahn Brothers in 1978,
adopting the teachings of Benjamin Graham as their investment philosophy. Managing more than $700 million as of the end of 2011, the company operates investment
management accounts on behalf of institutional and high-net-worth clients. The
company's mission is to provide clients with "superior returns on investment while
limiting their exposure to risk and to the potential for permanent loss of capital."*

*In line with its determination to remain a privately owned company, Kahn
Brothers looks to grow its client base and assets under management at a measured
and controlled pace, adding only those who share its long-term investment philosophy. Accordingly, the Kahns assure their clients that they have no interest in
ballooning assets for the sake of growth or to bolster the company's sales prospects.*

*In addition to managing Kahn Brothers, Thomas Kahn manages two private
funds and serves on the boards of Provident New York Bancorp, JBI International (the Jewish Braille Institute), the Ackerman Institute for the Family, and
the Jewish Guild for the Blind.*

35

When Thomas Graham Kahn was born in New York in 1942, his father Irving gave him his middle name in honor of Benjamin Graham, the "father of value investing." It is no surprise that young Thomas was thus brought up to think like a value investor.

Although he was raised in Belle Harbor, a middle-class neighborhood in the borough of Queens, Kahn knew that his father's financial independence had not come easily: "Irving started with nothing, but thanks to the fundamental analysis he learned from Ben [Graham], he was able to put what money he had to work by investing in the stock market wisely and intelligently." The younger Kahn learned early on that "it's important to have capital working for you instead of you working for it!"

Kahn recalled: "For my father, investing is not just a business, but also a hobby. I remember him coming home with a briefcase full of annual reports and reading them to me and my brothers, Donald and Alan, at the dinner table. On vacations, he always made sure that he had enough business and science materials to read, as he never read fiction. He taught us that if we wanted to control our destiny, we would have to delay immediate pleasures and save and invest wisely for the future."

Although he acquired his financial literacy from his father, Kahn owes his investment temperament to his mother, Ruth, who holds a Ph.D. in psychology from Columbia University. As the stock market is affected by human psychology, intelligent investing requires not only financial knowledge, but also the right mindset, especially in times of market frenzy and crisis.

Kahn elaborated: "There is nothing wrong with being an emotional person, but when it comes to investing, you need to set your own valuation standard. Then you also need to keep your emotions in check so that you are not affected by the general market. Sometimes, the best thing to do is nothing. But when the market is strong and everyone is telling you to buy, fighting temptation is easier said than done. Similarly, in a market crisis, when everyone is saying the stock market is dead, you need the courage to buy. In many ways, you need to train yourself to become a contrarian!

"Often going against the crowd, I have learned that successful investing is more art than science. If the investment game were all about numbers and calculations, then, in theory, given the computer programs available these days, you should be able to punch in the right criteria and make money all of the time. It doesn't work that way, however, so investing must be more of an art that involves having the right temperament and an understanding of companies."

Kahn always knew that he would eventually join his father in the investment field, but before doing so he decided to broaden his knowledge base by majoring in history at Cornell University in 1960. He believed studying political and financial topics would give him an understanding of the past and allow him to anticipate the future. Moreover, as history is the sum of human decisions and their consequences, its study affords a good sense of human psychology. As Mark Twain once said, "History never repeats itself, but it often rhymes."

Upon graduating in 1964, Kahn had two choices: Join the military and fight in Vietnam or, in lieu of military service, enroll in a government program to teach young children. Choosing the latter option, he taught at a public elementary school in the Bronx for several years. At the same time, he studied for an MBA at New York University's Graduate School of Business (renamed the Stern School of Business in 1988), completing it in 1967.

The following year, Kahn officially joined the investment industry, working alongside his father, Irving, and brother, Alan. He recalled: "I first worked with them at J.R. Williston & Beane and then at Abraham & Company. Initially, I was just a junior kid in the office, doing trade settlement recording. In those days, which came before the proliferation of computers, we had two stacks of index cards, one with client details and the other with the names of stocks. I had to write down what clients bought and sold on these cards, and then, when the market closed, I had to cross-check the data on the two sets of cards to make sure they matched.

"Recording trade settlements allowed me to learn about the companies our office followed, as well as our clients' investment habits and the types of companies they were interested in. After becoming more familiar with the investment business, I began to do some analytical work for my father."

Abraham & Company elected to be acquired by Lehman Brothers in 1975. Three years later, the Kahns decided it was time to launch their own investment firm.

Kahn explained: "Abraham & Company was a first-rate firm that was well capitalized and extremely well run. Before the acquisition, different investment teams managed clients' money. When Lehman came in, they wanted to put us all together to form a single team. We didn't like the new arrangement because the company had become too big. More importantly, our clients didn't like it either. They didn't want to deal with Lehman Brothers; they wanted to deal directly with the Kahns."

A Modified Graham Approach

Without doubt, Kahn Brothers' investment philosophy adheres closely to that advocated by Benjamin Graham, which can be boiled down to three words: "margin of safety." Graham wrote in *The Intelligent Investor* that "[to] have a true investment, there must be a true margin of safety. And a true margin of safety is one that can be demonstrated by figures, by persuasive reasoning, and by reference to a body of actual experience."

Although the Kahns' investment valuation model has evolved over time, Kahn explained, "We have never forgotten the importance of a margin of safety." In the company's early years, it looked for companies that traded below their net working capital (so-called net-nets). As these became more difficult to find in the 1980s, Kahn Brothers began to seek companies that sold below their private market or going-concern value.

"Nowadays, when people ask us about our investment strategy, I say we are 'modified' Graham investors," Kahn said. "Ben used to look mainly at the balance sheet, buying stocks that were trading below their net working capital. He never paid much attention to the nature of a business. Although we are similar to Ben from the mathematical standpoint, we have modified his teachings by also looking into the quality of a business and its assets. We often look at turnaround situations and often evaluate the true value of underpriced assets, such as land, intellectual property, and brand names.

"Like Ben, we look for discrepancies between pricing and valuation, but our definition of value and our expectation of the catalyst that will unlock that value are not always the same as those envisioned by Ben."

Although the firm has traditionally concentrated on small- and medium-cap companies, which are generally less followed by investors (and are thus more likely to be underpriced), Kahn Brothers is essentially an "all-cap" value manager. Kahn said: "If a stock sells below our calculated value and provides a comfortable margin of safety, then we are interested in learning more about it. Whether or not it fits into one of a consultant's 'investment categories'—large-cap, small-cap, emerging markets, etc.—is of less concern to us than finding strong, downside-protected investments wherever they may be.

"An important point to add is that we are also 'absolute' value managers. We never look at relative valuations. For example, we would never say that a company with 20 times earnings is undervalued simply because its peers trade at 30 times. Although we compare companies qualitatively, our main approach is to analyze their balance sheets, earnings, cash flows, and businesses. Hence, we would only say that a company is undervalued if it sells at a discount to what we determine to be an appropriate adjusted book value or trades below what we determine to be a conservative multiple of more normalized earnings. Importantly, we don't look at simple book value or simple price-to-earnings (P/E) ratios. We always make necessary adjustments and then evaluate the retooled numbers within the context of discussions with management."

Unlike the typical investor who heavily stresses a company's current earnings on its income statement, Kahn is more balance sheet–oriented. He believes that although earnings may have much to say about a company's prospects, they may reveal little about its corporate health. As a result, when he looks at a company's income, he focuses less on the current earnings and more on what earnings could be in a healthier environment in the future.

He elaborated: "Corporate health provides a much better margin of safety than good current earnings! We would rather invest in a company with a solid balance sheet, strong working capital, and little leverage than in a company with a lot of debt but strong earnings at present. In fact, we often favor companies that have near-term weak earnings or even no earnings but still have good corporate health because these types of companies offer better value.

"We call these companies 'fallen angels.' They are usually in good market and financial positions, but are suffering temporary problems.

If our research shows that such a firm has the capacity to fix its problems and improve earnings, then its share price should eventually rise again. If its problems persist and its earnings do not improve, then we will delve more deeply into its balance sheet to determine whether it has any valuable assets. These assets are sometimes so attractive that the company becomes a perfect takeover candidate."

In his search for fallen angels, Kahn often finds hidden gems. For example, some years ago he noticed that Thriftimart, a California supermarket chain, was sitting on valuable parcels of land in Los Angeles. As the reported value of this property was based on its historical cost, which dated back to the 1930s, investors had overlooked and underestimated its actual worth. Regardless of the nature of its business, the company was in fact a property investment play.

Holding Thriftimart stock for more than a decade, Kahn continued to add more shares whenever the share price dropped. He knew for certain that the company had little downside risk because its hard assets were worth much more than its share price indicated. When Thriftimart was eventually taken over, its annualized investment return was much greater than that for the Dow or Standard & Poor's 500.

Learning from this and similar investments, Kahn believes that patience and discipline are the keys to success. Investors must not be overly short-sighted in holding onto value stocks. Just because they fail to rise in price in a few months or years does not necessarily mean that they are non-performers. Indeed, value stocks often lag behind the general market for the majority of the holding period. Then, when their true worth is finally recognized, investors are often surprised at their attractive annualized investment returns relative to the broader market.

Kahn cited Syms Corp. as a more recent example. The company, which filed for bankruptcy protection in late 2011, sold discounted fashion brands. Although its retail business was losing money, Syms held properties across the eastern United States that were easily worth upward of $150 million. As its market capitalization was only half that, Kahn spotted an investment opportunity. Whatever the outcome of the liquidation proceedings, Kahn is certain that his downside risk is protected because of the firm's valuable real estate holdings.

"Undervalued stocks can remain underpriced indefinitely if nothing happens to them," Kahn noted. "We always ask ourselves what the catalysts are that can turn around these fallen companies. Coming up with the answer is a qualitative exercise that involves our experience, knowledge, and insights. There is no right or wrong answer to the question, but it is nevertheless an integral part of our research process."

In determining turnaround catalysts, speaking directly to a company's management team is often an effective strategy. Kahn added: "I like to talk to management, assess their abilities and personalities, and understand their way of thinking so that we are on the same page. I am always friendly, and my intention is to look them in the eye and get a good sense of their character. This may seem an old-fashioned way of judging people, but it's very effective."

Although Kahn Brothers always talks to the management teams of mid- and small-cap companies, listening to the conference calls and attending the analyst meetings of large-caps are generally sufficient, Kahn said. "Fortunately, we always have access to company management because we have been in the industry for a long time. Also, my father promoted corporate transparency by organizing analyst meetings for many different companies, and so we have gotten to know quite a number of people."

Although friendliness to management should be viewed as a strength rather than a weakness, the Kahns can be unforgiving when they find executives attempting to profit at the expense of shareholders. Kahn explained: "We have been involved in shareholder rights litigation in the past. My older brother, Alan, who is now retired from our firm, was quite active in the scene. Although I am less confrontational than he is, when management tries to harm shareholders, it is important to stand up for our rights!"

To minimize the chances of encountering such shoddy business dealings, Kahn prefers to invest only when he has the strong conviction that management's personal interests are aligned with those of shareholders. For example, he makes sure that executive pay is fair by industry standards and that top managers have a sizable portion of their net worth in the company through direct stock ownership rather than through the issuance of stock options or warrants.

Although Kahn recognizes that incentivized pay is currently fashionable in the corporate world and can be an effective tool if used correctly, he prefers managers who also choose to make direct purchases with their hard-earned money. Such hard-dollar purchases send the unmistakable message that management is confident in the future of the business and has long-term interests that are aligned with those of shareholders.

The Case for Obscure Securities

Kahn firmly believes that if a company has a clearly defined direction and good health and prospects, then it is far less likely that it will be underpriced in the first place. Therefore, value investors, in his view, are almost always contrarians who tend to analyze obscure securities that are ignored by the general market.

He explained: "Value investing is essentially a contrarian approach. It involves buying something that is currently unpopular and waiting for it to become popular again. It's like buying a long skirt at a thrift shop when miniskirts are in fashion or buying a heater in the summer and an air-conditioner in the winter."

A problem Kahn has identified in business schools is that students are taught simply to look for good investments with great prospects. If companies are already popular and have great prospects, however, then everyone would be smart enough to determine that, and their stocks would be trading at a premium. He elaborated: "We are uncomfortable about paying up for great prospects because we are unable to assess their downside risks. We would rather go in the other direction and look for companies that people feel terrible about and then analyze whether, from the perspective of a long-term investor, the negative sentiment is warranted. Doing so allows us to focus on the strengths of beaten-down companies and to assess how serious their downside risks really are.

"Investing is about finding opportunities that grow your capital, not necessarily finding companies that will grow. Sometimes you can grow your capital with non-growth companies. Being contrarians, we look for opportunities in less likely spots. Instead of asking what's right, we ask what's wrong. If the situation is not catastrophic, and the stock is selling at a deep discount, then we have limited downside risk and good upside potential. As Warren Buffett once said, 'Never count on making a good sale. Have the purchase price be so attractive that even a mediocre sale gives good results.'"

Kahn screens for such obscure investment opportunities in the traditional manner. He checks out the daily stock losers and 52-week lows in the newspapers or on his computer. He said: "Looking at the new lows and new highs informs you of market sentiment. It's not a high-tech way of looking for ideas, but it's one way of assessing the market that has worked for us for decades.

"On the losers' list, we often see stocks that have industry-specific issues that drive down share prices. In such cases, we quickly find out what's wrong in the industry in question, analyze the companies therein, and differentiate between the good and the bad. As there is nothing wrong with holding cash, if we feel uncomfortable with a company, then we pass and move on. In general, we like to pay attention to companies that create concerns among investors because they are more likely to be underpriced assets."

To get ideas, Kahn noted that the firm sometimes looks at the holdings of "friendly competitors," fellow value fund managers whose opinions he respects. He never pays attention to the stock recommendations of financial actors and television talking heads: "They are interested in fashionable stocks, and we are interested in those that are out of fashion!"

The trouble with today's lay investors, Kahn believes, is that they are all "experts": "It's the same as today's patients going to see a doctor. Before their appointment, they research their illness on the Internet and then advise the doctor on what medicine he or she should prescribe. Investing should not be like that. You need expertise and experience to look behind standard data and to uncover what others have failed to see."

Kahn cited the example of Voxx International, formerly Audiovox Corporation, a company that owns and distributes a variety of branded consumer electronics that it sells through major U.S. retailers, such as Best Buy and Wal-Mart. In 2005, the company received a NASDAQ delisting notice because it had failed to file its audited financial statements on time. Although many investors became skeptical of the company in the wake of the notice, Kahn was excited because he had identified an obscure opportunity.

He looked more closely into the company's financials, spoke to management, and learned that Voxx International was not permitted to employ its historical audited numbers due to an investigation launched by a prior auditor that the company was fully aware of. The delisting notice was thus fully anticipated, and the company regained its listing status once the situation had been resolved.

Kahn recalled: "The headlines sounded terrible, but if you looked into the company's earnings and financials, you could see that it was not at all affected by the delisting. If you knew why it was receiving the delisting notice, then you realized that you really had nothing to worry about. One point I would like to stress is that all of the information we looked at was in the public domain. It wasn't as if talking to management had given us the upper hand."

Taking a position in Voxx International and planning to hold it for the long term, Kahn Brothers displayed no hesitation in buying an even greater stake in the company when its stock tumbled drastically during the financial crisis in 2008. At the end of 2011, Kahn Brothers held close to 11 percent of Voxx International's total shares outstanding, becoming the single largest shareholder.

He explained: "The stock was beaten down to $6, although it had a tangible book value of $12, earned 75 cents, and had a cash flow of $2 per share. That's a value deal! Although we often tell our investors that our investment holding period is usually three to five years, when you find a value stock like that—where the company is doing everything right, its intrinsic value continues to improve, and its management is conservative and sophisticated—then our holding period can be much longer. After all, a stock represents a business, and we invest in businesses!"

Being value rather than momentum driven, Kahn noted, the firm often buys too early. "As contrarians, we never expect to time the market correctly because something that is out of favor tends to lag behind the market in the short term. Instead of going all in, we like to buy a small position in a company, get to know it better over time, and then accumulate our position gradually. In the case of Voxx International, we eased into our position over the course of two to three years."

This buying strategy naturally means that Kahn Brothers' best capital gains usually come from later purchases. The point, Kahn explained, is that "as long as we believe we know the situation, we are not afraid to average down on the prices of our stocks. As Ben [Graham] used to say, 'You are neither right nor wrong because the crowd disagrees with you. You are right because your data and reasoning are right.'"

Market Reflection

Kahn believes that emotional intelligence is crucial to becoming a successful investor. Although life experience is helpful in this regard, learning directly from someone who has survived good times and bad is indispensable. In Kahn's case, no one has provided a better example than his father, Irving.

He said, "One of the good things about investing is that there is no mandatory retirement age; you only get wiser as you get older. My father has gone through the best and worst of times in the stock market, and he has taught me to remain calm in both crises and frenzies. In fact, his presence also helps to calm our clients in times of uncertainty."

One of the most important lessons Kahn has learned from his father is that investing is all about consistency. Many fund managers may have produced good results for a few years, but then find their investment strategy no longer works. "True managers need to be tested in multiple business cycles to prove that their compound annual return is consistent over long periods of time," Kahn emphasized. "So, a consistent investment philosophy and strategy is essential. Of course, having good health, which allows you to remain in the game over the long run, is also important."

Again, Irving Kahn provides a case in point. "My father is now 106 and shows no signs of slowing down," the younger Kahn said. "He comes to the office to carry out research and talk to companies for about four hours a day, five days a week. Not bad at his age! Sometimes I will phone a company to chat with management, and they will tell me that my father beat me to it. My goal is to follow in his footsteps, and I too have no intention of retiring."

Another similarity between father and son is their devotion to reading. "I don't know of any successful investors who come up with good ideas without reading," Kahn said. "My father has read thousands of books and has a special interest in science. Because of his vast knowledge of the subject, he focuses on the future and rarely dwells on the past. He constantly looks forward to the technological break-throughs and good things that will happen to mankind in the future."

Although neither the financial crisis of 2008 nor the dot-com bubble of the late 1990s caused him undue concern, Kahn was disturbed by the so-called Flash Crash of May 2010, when the Dow plunged 1,000 points

in a matter of minutes. The cause of the crash, as an extensive exami-
nation by the Securities and Exchange Commission subsequently
showed, was unusually heavy selling on the basis of mathematical
algorithms by high-frequency trading firms.

Kahn commented: "The stock market is based on confidence. These
hyperactive algorithmic traders, who use mathematical programs and
technological tools to trade fleetingly in and out of the market to
generate profits, not only create huge volatility in the market, but they
also undermine the confidence of individual investors. They turn the
stock market into a casino."

Kahn is also bothered by the introduction of exchange-traded funds
(ETFs). "In the beginning, they were fine," he noted, "but as Wall
Street traders tried to gain a foothold in the business, they created
leveraged ETFs that allow market speculation. Because these ETFs
constantly need to rebalance their positions, they create unnecessary
swings for individual stocks. Now that stocks are rising and falling for the
wrong reasons, no one knows what's going on in the market anymore.
The situation is very harmful for those who wish to invest in good
companies for the long term."

Kahn looks back fondly to the days when brokerage firms charged
investors a fixed-price commission stipulated by the New York Stock
Exchange. Although the system had its problems, it nevertheless discouraged individual investors from excessive market trading. The removal
of the fixed-price commission in 1975 prompted the rise of discount
brokers and then electronic brokers, who encourage investors to trade
more frequently, thus leading indirectly to today's speculative market
environment.

"Now that frequent trading is in fashion, and serious long-term
investing has fallen out of favor, I am going against the crowd again," Kahn
concluded. "Although the excessive volatility in the market can harm
our portfolio in the short term, as long as we are disciplined and patient, it
also creates unique opportunities for us to buy stocks at even cheaper prices.
As long as we remind ourselves of the importance of a margin of safety
and of owning out-of-favor, value-oriented companies for the long term,
then our holdings will eventually become popular again."

CHAPTER 4

On the Shoulders of Value Giants

William Browne

Tweedy, Browne Company

Associate with men of good quality if you esteem your own reputation; for 'tis better to be alone than in bad company.

—*George Washington*

*W*illiam Hetherington Browne is a managing director and portfolio manager at Tweedy, Browne Company LLC. Founded in 1920, the company started life as a brokerage firm, then changed its business model in 1959 and began managing capital according to Benjamin Graham's value investing philosophy. In 1997, the estate planning needs of its partners prompted the firm to sell a 70 percent stake to the Affiliated Managers Group.

Working at Tweedy, Browne since 1978, Browne now has more than 40 years of investment experience. Managing directors Browne, John D. Spears, Thomas H. Shrager, and Robert Q. Wyckoff Jr. are responsible for the firm's $12.6 billion in assets under management.

At the end of 2011, approximately $6.6 billion of that amount was in managed portfolios for individuals, partnerships, and institutions. The remaining $6 billion was in offshore funds and four mutual funds. Both the employees and directors of Tweedy, Browne "eat their own cooking," with approximately $626 million of their own money invested in the company's own investment products.

Managing mutual funds since 1993, Tweedy, Browne currently offers the Value Global Fund, Value Global Fund II (currency unhedged), Value Fund, and Worldwide High Dividend Yield Value Fund.

Its most notable fund, the Value Global Fund, was launched in 1993 and had net assets worth $4.37 billion at the end of 2011. It has generated an annual *average return of 9.47 percent since inception. Over the same period, its benchmark index, the Morgan Stanley Capital International Europe, Australia, and Far East (MSCI EAFE) index, has returned an annual average of just 4.29 percent.*

"What is a stock?" asked William H. Browne. "Ask around and you get different responses from different people. To me, a stock represents an interest in a business! If you believe in this simple framework, then you will analyze and figure out the worth of a business before you make an investment decision."

Browne was born in 1944 and is one of the four sons of Howard and Katherine Browne. Although he learned the value of a stock at a young age, he had to embark on his own journey to truly understand the meaning of stocks and their worth.

"My father was a broker," he explained. "He worked at a brokerage firm that was founded by Forrest Berwind 'Bill' Tweedy in 1920. In 1945, when my father and Joseph Reilly were made partners, the company changed its name from Tweedy & Company to Tweedy, Browne and Reilly."

Browne grew up in the suburbs of New York City. Although his father owned a brokerage firm, the business was small and its income was modest. To earn pocket money, the young Browne ran around his neighborhood, collecting newspapers and selling them for recycling at a penny a pound. "My memories are generally pleasant," he recalled. "Unlike now, with many threatening events on your doorstep, we didn't get much news back then, except I remember the Korean War breaking out as a child, and my neighbor's son getting killed in the war."

From a young age, Browne frequently visited his father's office to listen to Wall Street stories. Then, as he grew older, he began working in the summer as a "runner" for his father's brokerage firm, carrying stacks of stock certificates and delivering them to other brokerage houses. On his way in and out of the office, he often bumped into many interesting figures, including the future richest man in the world, Warren Buffett.

In the 1940s and 1950s, the U.S. investment community was small, and individuals with similar investment mindsets—including the disciples of the "dean of Wall Street," Benjamin Graham—would often come together, forming close bonds. The environment was ripe for the entry of Tweedy, Browne and Reilly, the business model of which attracted the first group of value investors to Wall Street.

"In the 1920s, Mr. Tweedy focused on a niche market on Wall Street by acting as a broker-dealer for closely held and inactive securities," Browne said. "He believed that by concentrating on that market, he would have less competition in the brokerage business. He methodically built the business by attending the annual meetings of these companies and copying down the names and addresses of their shareholders. He would then mail them postcards introducing his business."

He continued: "Gradually, Tweedy became the last resort in the brokerage community to trade obscure securities. Their main characteristic was that they were extremely cheap by any measure, whether it be discount to working capital, price-to-book (P/B), or price-to-earnings (P/E). So, Benjamin Graham, with his philosophy of finding cheap stocks, became Tweedy's largest client because the brokerage firm had all of the connections to and held these stocks."

As the business relationship between Graham and Tweedy continued to strengthen, the brokerage firm even took over office space next to Graham at 52 Wall Street. That proximity meant the firm's young runner had less distance to cover when settling trades with its major client.

Browne recalled: "In 1955, when Graham decided to retire, his research analyst, Walter Schloss, decided to start his own fund. To keep expenses down, Walter subleased a very small desk at Tweedy. I remember his desk was between the front door and the water cooler. So, whenever someone wanted some water, Walter had to stand up.

"Around the same time, Warren Buffett also began working for Graham, and he would also come to my father's office to chat. In fact, when Warren acquired Berkshire Hathaway in the late 1960s, my father was the broker who carried out most of the trades."

Browne's litany of well-known investment personages does not stop there. He explained that another student of Graham's, Thomas Knapp, came to Tweedy around this time with an idea that altered the firm's business model for good: "He told my father and Reilly that the brokerage firm was sitting on some marvelous assets and had an excellent network to gather cheap stocks. Instead of being a pure broker, he said, the firm should gather some capital and start investing. Because the firm didn't have any theoretical investment framework to begin with, Tom brought his expertise. That was a watershed moment for the firm in 1959."

When Reilly retired in 1968, the firm changed its name to Tweedy, Browne & Knapp. Then, in the 1970s when it registered as an investment advisor and began managing money for individuals and institutions, it became simply Tweedy, Browne.

Browne capitalized on his indirect involvement with so many investment geniuses from a young age by embracing one of his father's mottos: "No one ever learned anything by talking." Indeed, Browne learned to listen and find out what investing really meant for these individuals.

Despite such knowledge, however, he confessed that he initially had no intention of practicing value investing. He explained, "I was in my early twenties, and I remember there was a big round table in the office, and there was one instance when I walked in and saw Warren Buffett, Charlie Munger, Tom Knapp, Walter Schloss, my father, and another Tweedy partner, Ed Anderson, sitting there and chatting. Because I was surrounded by all of these people who would talk value all day, the topic didn't really seem very exciting."

Obviously, Browne changed his mind after experiencing other aspects of the investment world as he grew older.

A Valuable Detour

Browne admitted that he certainly had no interest in investment as a young boy, unlike the young Warren Buffett, who began his investment career at the age of 11. Indeed, he found just hanging around or playing baseball to be more enjoyable pastimes.

After graduating in 1967 from Colgate University in New York, where he studied political science, Browne joined the Peace Corps, spending two and a half years in Ecuador working on projects to aid the poor. "My future was pre-determined after graduation," he explained. "Either I joined the military and went to Vietnam or I joined a govern-ment volunteer program such as the Peace Corps to do something else."

Upon his return to the United States, Browne decided to further his education. With no financial support from his parents, and with a wife in tow after marrying in 1970, Browne found a value deal in Ireland. He recalled, "A random person I met in Ecuador told me about a new MBA program that was starting up at Trinity College in Dublin. The tuition was only £200. I thought that was a good deal, and so I signed up."

After receiving his MBA in 1971, Browne returned to New York to officially look for work. Having no intention of following in his father's footsteps, he found a job as a financial analyst at the Bank of New York: "The learning experience there was of high quality. I learned so much about fundamental analysis and how to value companies. But I was young and impatient, and wanted to try something different, so I quit after a while and started working for a man called Jerry Tsai."

Jerry Tsai was a momentum-type fund manager at Fidelity Invest-ments during the go-go years of the 1960s when his investments in glamour stocks made him famous. In 1965, he started his aggressive growth fund, the Manhattan Fund, which raised hundreds of millions of dollars.

Browne recalled, "I was following him [Tsai] wherever he went, and I had no clue how he picked stocks. The job was quite a poor fit for me because his way was completely nonsensical to me, and is the complete antithesis of what I do today. It was then that I started visiting Tweedy, Browne during my lunch hour and listening to people dis-cussing their investment ideas, and the idea of value investing began to make more sense to me."

Leaving Tsai, Browne found another analyst job at Drexel Burnham Lambert, an investment bank that specialized in start-ups and distressed companies. It later became infamous for its activities in the junk bond market. Although the analytical experience there was different from what Browne had experienced working for Tsai, he still found Drexel's way of valuating companies incomprehensible.

In 1978, at the age of 34, Browne finally decided to stop exploring other parts of the investment world and joined the value camp by accepting a position at Tweedy, Browne. He first oversaw the trading and brokerage part of the business, as his father, Howard, was retiring, and then gradually took on a more analytical role in portfolio management. Browne eventually became a partner in 1983.

Statistics and Beyond

Practicing Benjamin Graham's principles at Tweedy, Browne in the 1970s, the investment team focused on finding "net-nets," which are stocks that sell below their working capital.

Browne explained: "Graham's approach was statistical. In his own time, he was called a statistician, whereas he would probably be a credit analyst in today's terms. His idea of value was simply a stock that met his statistical criteria, such as a stock trading at two-thirds its working capital or liquidation value."

An expert in this strategy is a man we have already met in this book: Walter Schloss. "I have known Walter almost all my life," Browne said. "He is such a unique investor because he used only Value Line for his investment research. It is unbelievable that he applied the same strategy for almost half a century and outperformed the market consistently."

Browne recalled that identifying net-net stocks was hard work in the early days: "Similar to Walter, one of our partners, Edward Anderson, who joined in 1968 and is now retired, tracked down every single stock in the *National Stock Summary* and *Polk's Bank Directory*, which were like the yellow pages for stocks, and would then look for value picks that provided a good margin of safety. With the introduction of computers, however, these net-net stocks became harder to find because the investment industry became more competitive, and these stocks provided a lesser margin of safety because more investors were finding them."

Entering the 1980s, the investment valuation model began to change. The rise of leveraged buyout (LBO) investment companies, which took on huge amounts of debt to take over businesses, took the concept of "value" to the next level.

"These LBO investors, who are basically the same as private equity investors today, looked for companies that had a sustainable income stream, no debt, and fair P/E multiples," Browne explained. "Although they took on a huge amount of debt to buy out these companies, because their businesses had a predictable cash flow they could eventually pay off the debt and generate good returns."

As Tweedy had a library of undervalued securities that fit their criteria, many famous LBO investors of the day came to the company looking for cheap businesses to buy. He recalled: "Our team sat down with them, listened to their strategy, and learned about their valuation model. They indirectly taught us a new way of thinking about stocks. Obviously, we were not interested in leveraging debt to buy stocks, but they showed us how much an informed businessman would actually pay for a company by analyzing its business quality and sustainability."

Having learned the business valuation model of LBO investors, Browne and his team began to look into companies' corporate structures as well as their business natures. He began to realize that good businesses can generate better long-term investment returns than companies that are "cheap" in a statistical sense.

In simple terms, the statistical method of evaluating a company involves analyzing its past and present performance, including the worth of its assets. The business valuation approach adds the company's future prospects for profit generation into the equation.

Contrary to Graham's strict method of classifying value, the new business approach also brings intangible assets such as drug patents, brand names, and pricing power into a company's value consideration.

Browne elaborated: "If you consider the statistical approach, you often find cheap companies whose value derives from a non-business source. Either they have a lot of cash, or they have valuable assets. In the old days, this strategy was good because these stocks were trading at huge discounts, but they are hard to come by these days unless there is a huge market correction. Besides, if these statistically cheap stocks don't offer good discounts, your investment return on them becomes so thin that when you sell, your silent partner—the IRS—takes part of your capital gains.

"What we learned is that if you buy a good and sustainable business, then over time the return of that business will do the natural compounding for you. It also means that you don't have to trade so often and can care much less about daily fluctuations in stock movement.

With that said, you first have to believe in the concept that a stock represents ownership of a business!"

Browne emphasized that "the beauty of finding a good business is that you can ride on it for a long time. Because a good business is organic, adaptive, and can reinvest its own profit, both its human and physical capital will bring value to your investment as long as it has a competitive edge."

Browne offered this simple example of a good business and a not-so-good one: "If you are in a business selling white paper for a dollar a pound, and your competitor sells it for a little less, I am probably going to do business with your competitor. But if you are selling me a glass of Johnnie Walker whisky for a dollar, and your competitor sells a glass of Uncle Joe's whisky for a little less, I am probably still going to buy the Johnnie Walker.

"Statistically speaking, if the stock of the paper company is selling below its working capital, in the old days we would have bought it if the discount was good enough. But today, we would rather pay a fair value for the Johnnie Walker business than the paper company because it has a competitive edge over the long term."

As Warren Buffett says, "It is better to buy a good business at a fair price than a fair business at a good price!"

Setting a Global Standard

Although it may seem that the valuation methodology used at Tweedy, Browne has changed since Benjamin Graham's days, Browne stressed that the firm's investment philosophy remains intact and that its framework still adheres closely to what Graham preached. There are two values for every stock, the first being the current market price and the other being the calculated value of the business, whether that value is calculated from the asset-related or business-fundamental perspective.

Browne also emphasized that he and his team still use the statistical approach to search for stocks. Stringent criteria that fit their value concept must be met before any further analysis takes place. These criteria include low P/E ratios, decent dividend yields, low price-to-sales ratios, or low price-to-cash-flow ratios. Although there is no set-in-stone definition of what "low" means here, it generally has to do with the historical average of valuation ratios or the growth prospects of the company and the industry.

After considering the statistics, Browne and his team delve more deeply into the corporate structure of a company of interest, which involves an evaluation of its equity and debt structure. Finally, they focus on the quality of its business and the strength of its management team. Indeed, over the years, the firm has developed an acronym for its analytical process: PUCCI, which stands for pricing, units, costs, competition, and insider ownership.

In a Tweedy, Browne study, titled "10 Ways to Beat an Index," the company lays out 17 standard earnings outlook/value questions for investors to think about. They include consideration of such issues as the outlook for pricing and units, gross profit margins as a percentage of sales, general expenses, operating leverage, pre-tax profit margin, one-time expenses or profits, goodwill, consensus earnings, growth prospects, cash management, investing activities, competition landscape, merger and acquisition potential, investment valuations, and insider ownership and activities.

Browne said, "People often think 'value' means that you go into a trash can and find some junk that has value. If you can pick it up for free and sell it for a dollar, then you have a value deal! I think this perception is insufficient, if not inaccurate, because if you think about real value, it is about buying a good business that does the long-term work for you!

"In essence, what we do is make sure we find stable businesses and that the price we pay for them is less than what they are worth. We have a systematic approach to finding them, and then a qualitative approach to evaluating them."

Although Browne and his team sometimes meet the management of a company they are interested in to get an indication of what they have done in the past and will do in the future, such meetings are not prerequisites to making investments, Browne said: "We care more about the nature of the business. I think Buffett said something very relevant in this respect: 'When a management with a reputation for brilliance tackles a business with a reputation for poor fundamental economics, it is the reputation of the business that remains intact!'"

In the early days, Tweedy, Browne invested only in American businesses. Around the mid-1980s, however, Browne and his team began to formulate the idea of investing globally.

He explained: "As we developed client relationships in Europe, mainly in the U.K., we shared our value concept with these foreign clients. Gradually, they began to recommend their own domestic stocks, and we began to keep track of them. With computers entering the picture later on, we had easier access to these foreign stocks, and so they naturally became an extension of our investment research. After all, we think the value approach is quite universal; it should not be limited to just one country."

A good example of Tweedy, Brown putting statistics, business valuation, and global investing to work is its purchase of the shares of Latin American bottler Panamco. First, the company met the statistical criteria set by the investment team. Second, its unique position in Latin America represented growth potential and a competitive edge. Finally, applying the business valuation approach, it could easily be taken over at roughly 10 times its valuation multiples.

Trading at $15 at the time of the first purchase, the stock soon tumbled, so naturally Browne and his team bought more. In 2003, Coca-Cola FEMSA bought the company at $22 a share, closely matching the takeover multiples Browne had expected.

Discussing Tweedy, Browne's investment strategy, Browne noted: "First, we are not afraid when a stock drops because, if it is a good business, we will want to buy more if we are in it for the long term.

"Second, going global was just a sensible extension to our business in the early 1990s. People now like to use the term 'globalization,' but long before this term came about, businesses had already become dynamic entities, maximizing profits and exploring opportunities intelligently in different parts of the world. Think IBM or Coca-Cola, which have gone to other parts of the world, understanding different cultures and allocating capital efficiently to where the growth is. At the same time, think of other global companies like Nestlé or Diageo, which are European companies that have come to America for businesses.

"Finally, it is important not to look purely at numbers. For example, if you looked at European banks in 2011, many of them would probably have fit our statistical standards on a P/B or P/E basis. The trouble was that you didn't really know what their assets were worth or what the variables were that could affect the industry going forward."

In this respect, Browne referred to Charlie Munger's two sets of folders: "the 'too-hard pile' and the 'take-a-second-look pile.' I think the concept of focusing on your strengths and your circle of competence is crucial when analyzing companies."

Browne pointed out that he has at times found himself at odds with analyst reports on companies. When analysts suggest that they do not like a company in the next six months or that it has no short-term catalysts but presents attractive opportunities for the long term, they are technically timing the market. Instead of trying to outsmart the market or time it, however, investing should be based on sound, objective reasons.

After all, in "10 Ways to Beat an Index," Tweedy, Browne presents empirical evidence to show that ('80 to 90 percent of investment returns have occurred in spurts that amount to 2 to 7 percent of the total length of the holding period.)The rest of the time, stocks' returns have been small."

The Social Science of Investing

Browne believes that investing is not a natural science, but a social science: "Investing is driven by people, and people are not rational most of the time! In investing, what you need to do is to find businesses that have high probabilities of surviving in the market. Then you implement a methodology to buy them at the right price so you can be more often right than wrong.

"Many people invest based on their intuition. They buy a stock because they think it's the right time or it's going up, but they have no grounds to support their thesis. What we do at Tweedy, Browne is about building an investment process. The ideals of the process are that it can be passed on, and it can be applied at any point in time and in different places because the logic is timeless and universal.

"Since business fundamentals, company management, or even government rules can change, fluctuations of stocks affect investors' emotions. Because of that, there is no such thing as an immutable natural law of investing; rather, there can be a process that the investor accepts and internalizes and upon which a compelling logic and understanding of investing can be built."

Although most investors enjoy the sizzling trends and excitement of the stock market, Browne speculated that perhaps value investors suffer from a rare psychological illness called ataraxia—a state of tranquility, characterized by freedom from worry or any other preoccupation.

He explained: "Value investors suffer from ataraxia because there is this sense of calmness and willingness not to pay attention to what others are doing. As you read the newspaper each day, you tend to be affected by the opinions and comments of others, but as a value investor, you must keep calm. Doing so requires a strong emotional and intellectual framework that anchors you to an objective way of looking for the right investments that fit your personality."

There is a saying that "when everyone thinks alike, everyone is likely to be wrong." To prevent thinking like and following the herd, Browne and his team embrace diversification and teamwork.

Browne believes that diversification, especially on a global scale, is the best way to minimize country- and business-specific risks. Unlike some investors who prefer a concentrated portfolio, he and his team prefer to convey to investors the message that nothing in the future can be certain. Diversification is a way of safeguarding against adverse movements in any particular investment holding.

"Some investors ask us why we would rather diversify into our twenty-fifth stock rather than put that money into our ten best holdings," Browne said. "The truth is, we really aren't certain enough to say which are our ten best, and so we would rather diversify.

"Besides, diversification allows us to be less obsessive with our holdings. Sometimes we find a good business for the long term, but its stock doesn't move in the short term. If an investor is too concentrated on a portfolio, he or she might overemphasize a particular position, making silly buy-and-sell decisions by focusing too much on the stock price and not on the business. With diversification, we can reduce such anxiety."

In value investing, there is the danger of what is known as the "value trap," which occurs when a beaten-down stock is mistaken for a value stock. When a value investor applies the statistical approach to finding bargains in the stock market, value traps often appear on his or her radar. To prevent falling into these traps, open discussion within the investment team is important.

Brown elaborated: "We have at least 13 to 14 analysts constantly looking for investment ideas. Each of our analysts has a different dimension to his or her background that allows us to look at different companies in different countries. Although we all share the same investment philosophy, we don't think alike, so when an idea comes up, we all sit down as a team and discuss it openly and critically."

Playing devil's advocate during brainstorming sessions not only allows the team to avoid value traps, but also prevents groupthink: "We try to be as objective as possible, and our team members can voice their concerns openly. That's how we learn and improve. Also, we try to be fair to everyone. If one analyst comes up with six ideas this year and another only two, that doesn't necessarily mean one is making more money than the other. We understand that industries go through cycles. What is important is that every analyst is well prepared because value may favor his or her sector at any time."

Indeed, when a good stock idea does come up, the four managing directors, including Browne, hold an open vote before any buying takes place: "Hypothetically, if it was a split vote, I would actually wonder why we had gone this far," Browne said.

"It's not like a blackball voting system, where one says yes and one says no. If an opinion is split, it is usually because some of us wish to get the stock at a cheaper price, or there is another investment alternative. The whole exercise is meant to encourage open discussion and to make sure we have a process, rather than buying stocks based on our intuition."

The Market Ahead

A value investor with a disciplined schedule, Browne wakes up each day at 5:30 A.M. After checking the latest news on his Bloomberg machine, he heads to the office at around 7:15 A.M. Leaving the office after the stock market closes at 4:00 P.M., he heads to the gym and exercises for an hour and a half before returning home. When the Asian market opens around 8:00 P.M., he occasionally calls his Asian affiliates to brainstorm ideas.

For Browne, keeping the passion for investing alive means keeping an active mind while learning about the world through business analysis. What displeases him about the market is the way in which the world is changing in the name of technology.

He explained: "The most incomprehensible time in my career thus far was the Internet bubble. The whole thing was nothing but air balls and promotions. That was a stressful time because all of the good businesses we liked were left behind, and anything related to the Internet went up every day. One investor wrote to us and said, 'Elvis Presley is dead. Wake up and face reality.' Obviously, our investment model was proven right when Internet stocks eventually collapsed."

In addition to the Internet boom, there is another technological advance in the stock market that also worries Browne. "The introduction of high-frequency trading and ETFs (exchange-traded funds) are making excuses in the market," he said. "People say they bring more liquidity into the market and improve the spreads of stocks. Well, we can have a long debate on that because to what degree liquidity and spreads are good for investors is subjective."

Browne believes that the problem lies in the way these financial products create inherent volatility in the market, which undermines its essential purpose: serving as a channel for capital allocation and a saving mechanism for investors.

He continued: "People in general are wired to be emotional and are not objective. When the market fluctuates so much in the name of liquidity and technological improvement, people panic, and what progress do we really see when many homes are taken away and savings are wiped out by these financial products?

"Besides, stock exchanges are now public companies. Serving in the best interests of their shareholders, their goal is to cooperate with institutions to promote products that require active trading. When an institution has to rebalance its ETF stock positions every day, commissions are generated. That means we see more trading and speculation even on good stocks, which fundamentally contravenes what people should be doing and how the market is supposed to serve us."

A discussion of the need for integrity and a more honest system on Wall Street inevitably calls to mind one highly respected figure: Walter Schloss.

"Walter is my role model," Browne said. "First, he never came close to any unclean dealings. Second, when he was managing his fund, he was well aware of his responsibility to investors, and so he protected them by keeping a focused strategy and not trying to lose money. When my father shared an office with him, I remember him once saying, 'If you ever have an argument with Walter Schloss, you are wrong because the man is packed with integrity!' People like him are in short supply these days."

Standing on the shoulders of value giants throughout his life, Browne has certainly learned the dos and don'ts of the stock market. No matter how the market will change in the future, the value philosophy will always serve as his last line of defense, not only as an investor but also as a person.

Browne will also continue to adhere to another of his father's mottos: "Friends and clients may forgive you for the silly mistakes you make in the stock market, but never for a dishonest mistake!"

CHAPTER 5

A Journey to the Center of Value

Jean-Marie Eveillard
First Eagle Funds

If you would be a real seeker after truth, it is necessary that at least once in your life you doubt, as far as possible, all things.

—*René Descartes*

*J*ean-Marie Eveillard is a French-born value investor who managed the First Eagle Global Fund (originally known as the SoGen International Fund) from 1979 to 2004. Over his 26 years of portfolio management, he generated an investment return of 4,393.08 percent, or 15.76 percent annually. During the same period, the Global Fund's benchmark index, the MSCI World Index, returned 1,514.25 percent, or 11.29 percent per annum.

In addition to First Eagle's notable Global Fund, Eveillard also managed the firm's Overseas and Gold Funds from their inception in 1993 until his retirement in 2004. The Overseas Fund, which invests in equities outside of the United States, returned 357.58 percent, or 14.36 percent per annum. Its benchmark index, MSCI EAFE, returned 83.54 percent, or 5.5 percent annually, during the same period.

Eveillard is highly respected in the investment industry, and his achievements were formally recognized by Morningstar in 2001 when he received its International Manager of the Year Award. In 2003 he was one of two recipients of the organization's Fund Manager Lifetime Achievement Award. According to Morningstar, the award "recognizes mutual fund managers who throughout their careers have delivered outstanding long-term performance, aligned their interests with shareholders, demonstrated the courage to differ from consensus, and shown the ability to adapt to changes in the industry."

Now semi-retired and living mainly in New York, Eveillard serves as senior advisor to and member of the board of trustees of First Eagle Funds and as senior vice president of First Eagle Investment Management, LLC.

Jean-Marie Eveillard confessed that he experienced 17 years of frustration before being able to practice value investing. After graduating from École des Hautes Études Commerciales—an esteemed French institution for the study of business—he joined Société Générale in 1962 as an analyst. At first, he was told to analyze stocks the "growth way," and it was not until 1979 that he was able to convince his boss to let him do so in the "value way."

Eveillard began his story: "When I first became an analyst in the 1960s, security analysis was a new concept in France and in continental Europe as a whole. Before that, it had been a matter of insider trading, stock tips, and rumors. By security analysis, I don't mean the Benjamin Graham approach. Instead, it was based more on the latest investment trend in the U.S., which was growth investing. The concept was to look for hot and momentum stocks rather than valuing their true business worth."

Before continuing, Eveillard stressed that a value investment is one that sells below its intrinsic value. In searching for such an investment, growth is always part of the calculation. The trouble is that the investment world has divided "value" and "growth" into two different camps, complicating the very essence of security analysis. To minimize confusion, he said he would nevertheless discuss "value" and "growth" as separate concepts to make his arguments easier to follow.

He resumed his story: "After six years at Société Générale, I became bored, and I thought of doing something else because I found growth investing unsuited to my style. I told my boss about it, and he asked me if I wanted to spend a few years in New York City to do something different. Being single, I said yes, so in 1968 I moved to the U.S. While the work environment was different, I was still told to analyze stocks the growth way, so in the end my job was the same."

During his next six years as liaison between the bank's New York City and Paris offices, Eveillard's main duty was carrying out research on

American companies with growth potential, namely hot and glamour stocks. Although he did not then know what a better way of investing might be, he felt that the growth method involved too many aggressive assumptions, leaving no room for error.

Searching for an investment approach that would fit his style, Eveillard came across the name Benjamin Graham. He recalled, "After moving to New York, I met some French students from Columbia University. One day while cycling with them in Central Park, I shared my frustration with growth analysis, and they told me to read the books published by former Columbia professor Benjamin Graham. I bought a copy of *Security Analysis*, and, after finishing it, I read *The Intelligent Investor*. Right away, I said, 'Voilà! This is the investment concept I've been looking for!'"

Quickly becoming a value advocate, Eveillard preached the gospel of *The Intelligent Investor* to his colleagues, but no one listened. Feeling alone in New York City, he requested a move back to Paris in 1974. Although the bank initially asked him to manage a small investment fund upon his return, senior management soon rescinded the offer.

The next four years back in France were among Eveillard's most miserable professionally. The only value advocate at Société Générale, he was forced to adopt the growth investing approach, although his heart remained true to the value investing philosophy. Finally, in 1979 he was given the chance to relocate back to New York City, and this time his new duties included managing a small global investment fund.

He joked, "My boss knew I wasn't too happy at work, and by sending me over to New York, he wouldn't have to listen to my talk about value anymore. I was assigned to manage the SoGen International Fund, which had only about $15 million in assets. Because the fund was so small, the head office in Paris didn't care much about it. In fact, I managed the fund all by myself until 1986 when management began to notice my performance. They acknowledged me because I started sending some nice dividends back to the head office."

Looking back today, Eveillard has no idea why value investing made so much sense to him right from the beginning. He commented, "I think Warren Buffett once said that value investing is a concept that you either understand right away, or you don't! Either you are a value investor, or you aren't! It is unlikely that a person would gradually be converted into one." Although the Frenchman may not know exactly why he is all about value, his upbringing perhaps provides a clue.

Valley of Tears

The son of a railroad engineer, Jean-Marie Eveillard was born in 1940 in Poitiers, west-central France, when half of the country was occupied as part of World War II. To escape bombardment in the city, the Eveillard family moved to a small village to the south of Poitiers: "We stayed with my grandparents during the war, and I have memories of troops coming in and out of the village and of some German officers occupying my great-aunt's house.

"The world was uncertain, but life moved forward. My mother gave birth to four of her five sons, including me, during the war, so life was eventful for our family. After the war, we moved to the French occupation zone in Germany because my father had to help fix the railroad network that was destroyed during the war."

Eveillard recalled a lesson learned during mass after his family returned to France when he was nine years old: "During their sermons, the priests would always preach to us that we are sinners and that we are weak individuals who live constantly in sorrow while on Earth. True happiness, therefore, would not come until we entered heaven. I recall the priests telling us that we all live in the 'Valley of Tears.'

"Knowing that the world would be a permanent disappointment, I never expected to be happy every day. What puzzled me after coming to America is that many people see psychiatrists because they are unhappy, but if you expect life to be unhappy to begin with, then you don't really need help. You just press on and move forward!"

Eveillard further applied this observation to the investment world: "I think one of the reasons I didn't enjoy growth investing was because it assumes the world to be perfect and certain, which it is not! Becoming a value investor allowed me to acknowledge the fact that I am uncertain about the future, so my priority is to avoid losing money, rather than to generate big returns.

"Now, if value investing works, which I think it does, then how come there are so few value investors out there? I think it has to do with human psychology. By being a value investor you are a long-term investor. When you are a long-term investor, you accept the fact that your investment performance will lag behind that of your peers or the benchmark in the short term. And to lag is to accept in advance that you will suffer psychologically and financially. I am not saying that value investors are masochists, but you do accept in advance that your reward, if any, will come in time and that there is no immediate gratification."

In many ways, Eveillard's childhood experiences groomed him into a value-oriented man. Reading Graham's *The Intelligent Investor* gave him the conviction and confidence to become a value investor, teaching him the importance of humility, caution, and patience.

He explained, "You need humility because you know you can be wrong, and when you admit that you stress caution by assigning a margin of safety to your investments so that you don't overpay for them. Finally, you need patience to wait until they play out because, as Graham said, 'In the short run, the market is a voting machine, but in the long run it is a weighing machine.'"

The Inefficient Market

When Eveillard began to manage money in 1979, he noticed that many investment funds had no clear investment framework. Their objective was to beat the benchmark index, but their way of doing so was to time the market by trading in and out of index component stocks. Distinguishing himself with a value strategy, Eveillard went against the crowd to look for undervalued stocks that others overlooked or ignored.

"The search for undervalued stocks begins with the idea that stocks are not just pieces of paper that are traded in the market. Every stock represents a business, which has its own intrinsic value. To determine that value, you have to estimate what a knowledgeable buyer would be willing to pay for the business in cash. It is important to understand that intrinsic value is not an exact figure, but a range that is based on your assumptions. Because you have to revise your assumptions from time to time to reflect business and market conditions, intrinsic value fluctuates over time, and it can go up or down," he explained.

Eveillard admitted that he was rather lucky in his timing. When he took over the SoGen International Fund, stock markets were generally beaten down after the global sell-off in the 1970s. In the beginning, his main strategy was to apply the Benjamin Graham approach: "I looked at stocks in both the U.S. and Europe. Instead of focusing on how the economy in each was likely to fare, I focused mainly on stocks that were trading at 30 to 40 percent below my intrinsic value calculations. Because the Graham approach is mostly mathematical, I sat in the office all day trying to determine companies' liquidation value or net working capital from their balance sheets."

The first opportunities came from the United States, where both small- and large-cap stocks were beaten down. Then, as the U.S. market began to recover in 1982, value started to appear in continental Europe.

Eveillard recalled, "European small-caps were selling at ridiculously low levels by Graham's definition. I think one reason they were cheap was that continental Europe had a less transparent financial disclosure environment than the U.S., and therefore the market was less efficient.

"Speaking of efficiency, my experience also makes it difficult for me to believe in the efficient-market hypothesis, which posits that it is impossible for investors to beat the market because stock prices are always fair and reflect the most up-to-date information available to them."

Discussing some of the inefficiencies that exist in the European market, Eveillard mentioned that during his college years, he worked at a magazine called *La Vie Française*, a publication somewhere between *Barron's* and *Businessweek*. During his time there, he noticed that the journalists liked to speak favorably of big companies that advertised in the publication and less favorably of smaller non-advertisers, a situation that created price discrepancies between large- and small-cap stocks.

He also observed that some companies were inclined to report earnings that closely matched their dividend payments because the labor union would go after management if the company generated too much profit. Misreported earnings thus led to inaccurate evaluations of many European businesses.

Finally, Eveillard found some companies simply hostile to potential investors, making their annual reports or related filings difficult to access. If public information was not very public, he questioned whether the market was truly efficient.

He explained, "Applying the Graham model, I focused on hard and real assets. If they were selling at huge discounts to their stock prices, then I would buy. Eventually, as financial reporting became more transparent, these small-cap stocks went up in value.

"In the 1980s, some fund managers questioned me for buying these small-cap stocks because, if my fellow fund managers did not buy them, then they could hardly go up in value. Maybe they were right, but I believe that if a stock is cheap, then investors will eventually recognize its value. It may take three years, five years, or even longer, but the truth is that investing requires patience, and you need a huge amount of it to see good things happen!"

The Graham method of searching for undervalued stocks proved to be profitable, but as the world became more "efficient," the strategy became less competitive. Fortunately, in the late 1970s, Eveillard came across the name Warren Buffett and had the opportunity to read many of his Berkshire Hathaway annual reports. He then began to put the Buffett approach to use in the mid- to late 1980s.

Eveillard said, "Value is a big tent. You have Graham, who does it mathematically, and you have Buffett, who made a substantial adjustment to Graham's teaching by looking not just at the numbers, but also at the long-term prospects and quality of the business. The Graham approach was less time-consuming, and so I could work on the numbers on my own. Toward the end of the 1980s, I began to hire analysts so we could apply the Buffett approach. Having more people allowed us to spend a lot of time trying to find out the major characteristics of businesses and their sustainable competitive advantage—what Buffett calls a 'business moat.'"

Although he broadened his investment research, Eveillard stressed that in this period he remained a bottom-up investor who focused primarily on the intrinsic value of a business. However, he then also began to keep an eye on the top-down, so he looked at the macroeconomic environment of different countries: "We could ignore the economics of the more developed markets, but as we moved into analyzing emerging markets, we had to keep an eye on the bigger picture.

"Some emerging market stocks in Asia presented extraordinarily attractive valuations in the 1980s, but some of their respective countries were rife with political and economic instabilities, and so we had to be extra careful. In addition to understanding businesses, we also had to make sure their accounting systems were honest, as we had learned from experience that the numbers can't be trusted if management intends to mislead investors."

Speaking of accounting, Eveillard regrets that the accounting standard in developed countries became worse than those in emerging countries in the 1990s. He said, "Somehow, the integrity of accounting changed. When the economy was growing and every business was successful, the chief financial officers of virtually all large corporations in the U.S. began to think that they wouldn't go to jail for being intellectually dishonest because everyone was doing it, and so they started manipulating the numbers.

"I always start off my research by reading companies' annual reports and then the footnotes to their numbers. I need to be satisfied about the integrity of the numbers and the honesty of the accounting before I look further. If there is any number that is incomprehensible, I throw the report into the wastebasket and move on. If you look at Enron's footnotes in the 1990s, they were just incomprehensible. If investors had read those footnotes carefully, I don't think anyone would have invested in Enron stock."

The trouble with American accounting, according to Eveillard, is that it has extremely detailed rules. Good lawyers and CFOs will not get caught if they can find a way to work around those rules and manipulate the numbers. In Europe, however, accounting is more principle-based. Thus, one would violate the accounting system simply by betraying its fundamental spirit.

Regardless of which accounting standard is in place, Eveillard believes that the most important exercise for potential investors is to read through companies' annual reports and never take any numbers for granted. Successful investing is not just about achieving stellar returns, it is also about avoiding losses. When the numbers appear questionable, the best practice is to forgo the opportunity and look for the next one.

The Meaning of Value

When a company's financials make sense to Eveillard, his next step is to value the worth of the business: "We don't do much discounted cash flow analysis because it gives you an impression of worth down to the decimal point, which does not require being so precise. Instead, we prefer using EV/EBIT (enterprise value/earnings before interest and taxes) because it introduces the balance sheet to the multiples. The main goal of the analysis is to find out approximately how much the business is worth, in a reasonable range, if a knowledgeable buyer were to take over the company.

"By using EV, we include both cash and debt in the calculation, which is better than just looking at market capitalization. Then, with EBIT, we see how much interest the company is paying. Since we prefer companies with little to no debt, we expect minimal interest expenses. Then tax is also a concern because if a company pays a lower tax rate than its peers, we have to find out why. If there is no valid reason for a lower tax rate, then either the company is cheating the tax authorities or it is overstating its profits."

After a business is valued, the next step is qualitative analysis. This exercise focuses on the strengths and weaknesses of the business, not from the standpoint of whether the company can increase sales or earnings over the next quarter or two, but from whether it has any sustainable competitive advantage over the next five to ten years.

Eveillard commented, "After I retired in 2006, I helped teach a value investing course at Columbia University. I had about 12 students, and what struck me was that 11 out of 12 thought qualitative analysis had to involve 25 pages of writing. What I tried to stress to them was that they needed to think hard and then list no more than three to four strengths and weaknesses of the business.

"Besides, some of the best analysts I have dealt with have enjoyed explaining complicated situations and how a company could turn itself around and so forth. I always tell them that they are smart, but the more complication they try to read into the story, the higher the probability that they will make a mistake. I tell them that there is nothing wrong with making money through simple investment ideas. After all, that's what Warren Buffett has done for years. As he has said, he doesn't jump over seven-foot bars; he looks for one-foot bars that he can easily step over!"

During his investment career, Eveillard made it a point never to speak to company management until after he had done his homework. If the first question he asked gave management the impression that he knew nothing about the company, then they would have a greater tendency toward painting a good picture of the company.

Instead of asking questions about the company's latest earnings outlook or long-term strategic plan, Eveillard's goal was always to get a sense of the management team's personality. He explained, "There is no point asking about a company's earnings outlook because if we are investing for the long term, then short-term earnings never affect our intrinsic value calculation. Asking management about long-term plans is also pointless to me because the world changes. No one can predict what will happen, and so what is more important for us as analysts is to discover the underlying strengths and weaknesses of the business ourselves."

Because the world is uncertain, Eveillard has never believed in a concentrated investment portfolio: "I think a concentrated portfolio is more of a bull market phenomenon. In a bear market, if you are too concentrated, you never know what can happen to your stocks. Some people have asked me whether I just invest in my best ideas, but the truth is that I don't know in advance what my best ideas will be, so I'd rather diversify. Besides, the beauty of our global fund was that we could invest internationally, which helped to minimize country-specific risks. With that in mind, I am not saying that you should diversify the portfolio to the extent of creating a quasi-market index."

As his investment horizon has always been at least five years, Eveillard has never minded buying a stock on its way down. In fact, he believes that if a value investor has performed his or her calculations carefully, then a falling stock represents a good opportunity to load up with more. The only worry, then, is the fluctuation of intrinsic value over time because business conditions change.

He explained: "We don't set a specific target price for our stocks, but we monitor their intrinsic value closely because businesses can be better or worse than expected. We also read a lot of analysts' reports to get updates on businesses, but we always calculate their intrinsic value on our own. The trouble with analysts' reports is that their time frame is usually six to twelve months, but ours is five years. So, it is fine to read what they say about businesses, but not their target prices."

Eveillard does not believe in the existence of a "value trap." He does, however, believe in what Martin Whitman of the Third Avenue Value Fund said about the difference between a temporary unrealized capital loss and permanent capital impairment.

If a stock is worth \$70 and is currently trading at \$35, it is a value stock. If after a year the stock drops to \$25 but, based on prudent assessment the value investor believes that it is still worth \$70, he or she should not panic because the stock is simply going through a temporary unrealized capital loss. As long as the investor is patient, the stock will eventually reflect its true worth.

Permanent capital impairment, in contrast, is a pure mistake. It occurs when the value investor misjudges the strengths and weaknesses of a business and comes up with a deteriorating intrinsic value. Then the loss is not temporary, but permanent. Hence, the value investor should quickly cut the loss, learn from the mistake, and move on.

Eveillard further elaborated: "I think traders and speculators call it a value trap because their holding period is too short. If the intrinsic value of a stock remains unchanged, then even if its price goes down, it is still a value stock. You can't say that it is a trap just because your holding period is mismatched with the time it takes for the stock to recover. If you have patience, and if your analysis is right, then the market will acknowledge the stock eventually!"

The Courage to Say No

Although patience is required for value stocks to blossom, the value investor also needs the courage to say no, especially in times of market frenzy.

"Sometimes in life, it's not just about what we buy, but what we don't buy," Eveillard explained. "Because I became worried about the Japanese stock market in the late 1980s due to its gigantic credit boom, we sold all of our Japanese stocks in mid-1988. Some investors questioned us for pulling out from the second largest stock market in the world, but I said it's better to take some money off the table than to participate in market mania. Obviously, I was wrong and unhappy in the next 18 months because the market went up another 30 percent, but in 1990 when the market collapsed, we owned nothing in Japan and our decision was proved logical."

In the late 1990s, a similar situation occurred in the United States. This time it was technology, media, and telecoms mania. Eveillard's performance lagged behind that of his peers and the major market indices for three years, but he continued to say no to the market.

He explained, "If you lag in the first year, your clients are okay with it; if you lag again in the second year, they get nervous; and if you lag in the third year, they are gone! Our fund had total assets of around $6 billion in 1997, but by 2000 it was down to $2 billion. I was unhappy, but I constantly reminded myself that I was acting in the best long-term interests of our investors, so I had to do the right thing. When the mania was over, investors came back and praised our discipline. The fund [the First Eagle Global Fund] today has a size of close to $30 billion."

In the 2000s, Eveillard stayed away from financial stocks because the easy credit and low interest rates that prevailed reminded him of Japan in the late 1980s. He noted that both the U.S. and European banking industries had been highly regulated in the 1960s and 1970s. In those years, bank stocks traded at slightly below their book value and yielded around 4 to 5 percent. In effect, they were as boring as utility stocks. In the 1990s, however, the regulations changed, and banks began selling investment products and structuring exotic deals. As they began to generate hefty profits, Eveillard became wary of the industry's structure.

"First, the financial sector became bloated. Then, with the easy monetary policy and overall prosperity in the 1990s, which became even more amplified in the 2000s, the market became extremely risky," Eveillard said. "My worry was supported by the Austrian School of economics, which suggests that monetary authorities should be careful not to let a credit boom go on too long and become too strong because a credit bust naturally follows a boom, just as night follows day.

"The problem is that no one was listening to the Austrian School because post–World War II economics had been dominated by two economists: John Maynard Keynes and Milton Friedman. Since the two were friends with many politicians, and could offer solutions to many economic issues, they became more accepted.

"The Austrian School, on the other hand, provided hopeless messages by saying that the world cannot do much as credit boom turns to credit bust. Time is the only healer of any economic problem. It also suggests that any attempt to patch things up in the short term runs the risk of negative unintended consequences in the medium to long term.

"With quantitative easing by central banks and increased government spending to stimulate the world's economy after 2008, low interest rates have continued. If the Austrians were right, everything will be fine in the short term, but the unintended consequence will be higher inflation in the medium to long term. We have to remember that inflation is not asset prices going up or an increase in the consumer price index or commodity prices. It is just a symptom! Inflation is the excessive supply of money and the creation of credit!"

With the dynamics of the financial world changing since 2008, Eveillard has two pieces of advice: Look for a career outside the financial markets and seek refuge in gold.

He shared the story of renowned Austrian economist Ludwig von Mises, who declined an offer to work at a bank in the 1920s and continued to teach at Vienna University instead. His fiancée asked him why he had turned down such a highly paid job, and his answer was that the excessive credit boom of the 1920s would naturally be followed by a bust. Therefore, the last industry in which a person should wish to work would be banking. Fast-forward to the 2000s, when Eveillard's daughters asked their father why he had never pushed them into the finance industry, he told them the same story.

With regard to gold, Eveillard believes it to be an essential asset class in good and bad times alike.

Seeking Protection

As a value investor, Eveillard has never claimed to know the intrinsic value of gold, although his extensive reading about the failure of fiat money throughout European history makes it natural for him to speak positively about the yellow metal. After all, in an age of uncertainty, gold always provides protection and insurance against extreme outcomes.

In 1993, Eveillard set up the First Eagle Gold Fund on the assumption that there would continue to be an imbalance between the annual supply of and demand for gold.

He explained, "I set up the gold fund six or seven years too soon because I thought the downside was protected due to the imbalance of supply and demand, and I thought that the upside would take care of itself at some point. What I didn't understand was that supply and demand don't matter; what matters is whether there is investment demand. Obviously, the lack of demand at the time did not drive up prices. The fund started out with $50 million and was down to $15 million by the end of the 1990s. Now [2011], it is worth a little over $3 billion thanks to investment demand."

Eveillard argued that gold has no intrinsic value, just as paper currencies such as the U.S. dollar, euro, or Japanese yen have no intrinsic value: "Gold is a substitute currency. Because there is too much paper money and too little gold out there, every major currency became suspect after the 2008 financial crisis, and the alternative was to have some allocation of gold. As gold prices can easily fluctuate by a couple of hundred dollars, investors need to be careful even if their aim is to seek protection."

To illustrate the failure of fiat money, Eveillard cited a few historical incidents. For example, in 1716, when France found itself in financial ruins following the numerous wars launched by King Louis XIV, John Law, the country's controller general of finances, decided to issue paper money backed by coinage to repay the country's unsustainable debt. He continued to print money, made it illegal for French citizens to hold more than a certain amount of gold and silver, and devalued the country's banknotes relative to foreign currencies to improve exports. The schemes eventually led to public retaliation, and, in 1720, the paper money system collapsed and the once-celebrated John Law had to flee the country.

Eveillard also mentioned 1790 when, after the French Revolution, the French Assembly confiscated church lands and used them to back a new type of paper currency called the assignat. Initially issued with 400 million livres, by 1795, its total circulation had reached 40 billion livres, causing rampant inflation and public outcry. When Napoleon entered the scene, he introduced the gold franc, which was backed by gold alone. Only then did France's financial situation stabilize, and his reign was secured.

In more recent times, the Treaty of Versailles imposed punishing financial reparations on Weimar Germany after the end of World War I. To pay down its war debt, the country had to print money, but the more it printed, the faster the value of the mark dropped. Germans initially reacted to the resulting higher prices by economizing on their consumption, but when the value of the mark dropped faster than they could consume, they spent their paper money as fast as they could, causing hyperinflation in the 1920s. Many historians argue that the situation led indirectly to the rise of Hitler, the aftermath of which was World War II.

Eveillard said, "We Europeans learned long ago that paper money doesn't work! In the U.S., the pure paper money system is only around 40 years old since Nixon closed the gold window in 1971. With the excessive amount of money printed since the financial crisis in 2008, paper money is fraying at the edges. Now we have too much paper money chasing too little stuff, with the stuff being gold!"

His personal savings are invested in both the First Eagle Global Fund and the Gold Fund, as Eveillard knows that value stocks and gold will make good companions in the years to come. Reaching the age of 65 in 2004, he decided to retire because, as the French say, "*Il y a un temps pour tout* [there is a time for everything]!"

In their travels in Europe and the United States following Eveillard's retirement, he and his wife, Elizabeth, came to appreciate fine art and gradually began to collect drawings. In the midst of their search for their next piece of art, Eveillard received an unexpected phone call in 2007: His successor at First Eagle Funds had stepped down, and the Frenchman was asked to come out of retirement to oversee the transition to a replacement. "At first, I thought I would just be around for a few months, but it took much longer to find a replacement, so I ended up staying for two years," he recalled.

Officially free of major responsibilities since 2009, Eveillard continues to serve as a senior advisor to First Eagle Funds. Although traveling and art collecting are now his major retirement hobbies, he continues to keep track of the financial markets and occasionally discusses the failings of the global economy in business magazines and on television.

Speaking of the future, Eveillard concluded, "The key question today is this: are we still in the post–World War II economic and financial landscape, or have things changed as a result of the financial crisis in 2008? I don't pretend to have the answer to this question, but as the future is uncertain, my advice is to remember the importance of a margin of safety. As a value investor, you can be bottom-up all you want, but remember to pay some attention to the top-down because government policies are having a severe impact on the health of the world's financial markets."

CHAPTER 6

The Self-Taught
Value Spaniard

Francisco García Paramés
Bestinver Asset Management

When you have eliminated the impossible, whatever remains, however improbable, must be the truth.

—*Sir Arthur Conan Doyle*

*F*rancisco García Paramés is the chief investment officer of Bestinver Asset Management, a wholly owned subsidiary of Spanish industrial conglomerate Acciona, S.A.

Incorporated in Madrid in 1987, Bestinver originally managed the wealth of the Entrecanales family. Joining the firm in 1989, Paramés gradually took Bestinver to the next level by setting up its first equity fund, Bestinfond, in 1992. Then, in 1997, Bestinver launched a global equity fund called Bestinver Internacional.

Managing Bestinver's funds single-handedly until 2003, Paramés has generated stellar investment results not only within the Spanish community but within Europe as a whole. From Bestinfond's official launch on January 13, 1993, the fund returned 1,447 percent, or 15.76 percent annually, until 2011. Its benchmark index, the Madrid Stock Exchange General Index, returned 329 percent, or 8.10 percent annually, during the same period.

Bestinver's other notable fund, Bestinver Internacional, which was launched on December 31, 1997, had generated 221 percent, or 8.85 percent per annum, as of 2011. Its benchmark index, the MSCI World Index, dropped 2 percent, or −0.15 percent annually, during the same period.

Managing approximately €5.4 billion, or $7.4 billion, as of 2011, Paramés now works closely with two other fund managers, Álvaro Guzmán de Lázaro Mateos and Fernando Bernad Marrase.

Investing is about common sense. Charlie Munger, vice chairman of Berkshire Hathaway, once said, "All I want to know is where I'm going to die, so I'll never go there."

The same concept applies to investing. Spanish investor Francisco García Paramés believes that "an investor doesn't need to make personal investment mistakes to find out what doesn't work. What's needed is to read about others' mistakes and never follow them!"

A self-taught value investor, Paramés joined the investment management industry by chance.

Born in the north of Spain in the Galician city of A Coruña in 1963, Paramés is the second youngest of five children and the only son in the family. When he was young, he had little idea of what he wanted to do in life. If he had to pick a career during his teenage years, however, he would have chosen to play basketball professionally, and he remains a big fan of the NBA in the United States.

With an open mind about his future, Paramés attended Complutense University in Madrid, where he studied economics because the subject seemed much broader than others, such as law or accounting.

He recalled: "I didn't know anything about business until my third year in college, when I started reading *Businessweek* magazine to catch up on business news and improve my English. Having learned what companies do, in my last year of college I began working at Spanish department store El Corte Inglés doing paperwork for the purchasing department, which technically involved filing import and export documents for merchandise.

"Because I really didn't know what to do after graduating in 1987, I decided to study for an MBA at the IESE Business School in Barcelona. Around the time I finished my MBA in 1989, the school had a job recruitment day. Bestinver was there, and I was hired on the spot as an investment analyst."

Paramés admitted that he knew little about the role when he joined Bestinver. However, having evaluated his strengths and weaknesses and feeling fairly certain of what he should not do, if not what he should, he liked the sound of a career that required him to be analytical more than one in some other business area, such as sales and marketing. As a self-described "quiet person," an opportunity to be analytical seemed well suited to his personality.

In 1989, Bestinver was still a relatively small division within the Entrecanales' business empire. Paramés recalled, "Basically, it was just me and my boss. We were supposed to analyze merger and acquisition opportunities in Spain, but such activities slowed down shortly after I joined. To keep myself occupied, I began to analyze Spanish stocks. Because my boss had a very value-driven mindset, his fundamental approach provided me with a good investment framework, and fortunately I was pointed in a sensible investment direction."

Early in his career, Paramés noticed that investing constitutes value seeking in the first instance. Moreover, he observed that financial institutions distinguish between the concepts of "growth" and "value," probably for marketing purposes.

As a European who had read extensively about the rise and fall of many family empires within the region, he realized that those that weather crisis after crisis are the ones that look for investments with sustainable growth and value over the long term. If these empires had been speculative and myopic to begin with, then how could their legacies have lasted for centuries?

Indeed, Paramés's fundamental investment beliefs were confirmed by Warren Buffett when he wrote in his 1992 annual letter: "In our opinion, the two approaches [value and growth] are joined at the hip: Growth is always a component in the calculation of value, constituting a variable whose importance can range from negligible to enormous and whose impact can be negative as well as positive . . . In addition, we think the very term 'value investing' is redundant. What is 'investing' if it is not the act of seeking value at least sufficient to justify the amount paid?"

When his boss left Bestinver in 1991, young Paramés was on his own in the research department. He said, "I learned about value from my boss, but more importantly, my investment framework was further consolidated after reading the book *One Up on Wall Street* by Peter Lynch. I still remember when the book came out in 1989, and I read a review in *Businessweek*. I went out and bought it, and it changed my life forever."

Among the words of wisdom that struck Paramés in reading *One Up on Wall Street* are these: "Stock prices often move in opposite directions from fundamentals but long term, the direction and sustainability of profits will prevail. It takes remarkable patience to hold on to a stock in a company that excites you, but which everybody else seems to ignore.

You begin to think everybody is right and you are wrong. But where the fundamentals are promising, patience is often rewarded; it's only by sticking to a strategy through good years and bad that you'll maximize your long-term gains."

Paramés added, "I think I had the value gene in me to start with, but Lynch's book really reinforced and developed my investment logic. After Lynch, I read all of the books that I could find on value investing. Just a few of the investors I read about were Warren Buffett, Benjamin Graham, John Neff, Sir John Templeton, Walter Schloss, and Philip Fisher. With little pressure on me from the Entrecanales family in my first two years of employment, I was fortunate to be able to learn at my own pace."

On a Solo Value Hunt

After his boss's departure from the firm, Paramés asked the Entrecanales family whether he could continue to run Bestinver's portfolio on his own. To his delight, they approved his request. He explained, "In my first two years of doing investment analysis, I was convinced that a prudent manager could definitely add value to a portfolio to improve investment returns. I have always been shy, but somehow I was quite confident about what I was doing, so I had the courage to ask. I am grateful to this day that they let me run Bestinver's funds on my own.

"Bestinver had a capital injection of about €10 million to begin with. This was a lot to me, but not a huge amount for the Entrecanales family. Because the family put little pressure on me, I could really focus on value, think for the long term, and put my investment principles to work. I knew that if I could build up a nice track record, I would eventually be given the chance to build something bigger."

Because he was able to do something on his own at such a young age, Paramés now advises young people to start investing as early as possible. What is important, he believes, is to have the right investment mindset and to build a track record no matter how large or small the size of the portfolio: "If the investment logic is sensible and the record is acceptable, then you will be recognized over time."

Paramés vividly remembers his very first investment research, which was on the Acerinox Group, a steel company in Spain. His work showed him the cyclicality of businesses and the way in which they go through peaks and troughs along with the economic cycle. Being a prudent investor requires patience and discipline because it is easy to get carried away in a bull cycle or overly discouraged in a bear cycle.

Paramés early on took Sir John Templeton's words to heart: "The four most dangerous words in investing are: 'This time it's different!'"

Discussing the first investment he ever made, Paramés recalled, "I was about 27 years old at the time, and I bought into the Spanish bank Banco Santander. This was before the Persian Gulf War in 1990, and stocks were quite beaten down. My position dropped 30 percent over the next two years, and I bought more. Six years later, I sold it and made a nice gain. This was the only time I used leverage to buy a stock, and I remember borrowing around €20,000 from my father and friends."

Paramés further added that Banco Santander was one of the very few personal stock investments he has ever made because when Bestinver officially launched its own fund in 1993, he began to put all of his personal savings into the fund to align his interests with those of his investors.

Although he made money with Banco Santander, Paramés learned two important lessons. The first was that bank stocks are too difficult to understand. In the early 1990s, Spanish banks had loan-to-deposit ratios[1] of 50 to 70 percent, which was both conservative and healthy. But by the mid- to late 2000s, those ratios were nearly 150 percent.

With so much leverage in the system and with bank assets so difficult to evaluate, Paramés decided not to touch the sector again unless the situation changed. Banks continued to over-leverage themselves, and he continued to stay away. When the financial crisis hit in 2008, Bestinver was not as badly affected as many other investment funds that had exposure to the financial industry.

"The second lesson I learned," Paramés said, "is not to use leverage because anything can go wrong. It's normal for a 25-year-old or a 30-year-old to leverage up on an investment because a young person

---

[1] The loan-to-deposit ratio is used to assess a bank's liquidity by dividing its total loans by its total deposits. If the ratio is high, the bank is over-leveraged and has little liquidity to cover its funding requirements; if it is too low, the bank is not fully maximizing its earnings potential.

always wants to get rich quickly. But after reaching a certain age, one begins to realize that it is harder to make up for losses than to protect against them, and so the whole investment game is about quality and sustainability."

What matters most in the process, he continued, "is to find value stocks with good positions in the marketplace because they will be around for a long time. Peter Lynch's motto is very true: 'Go for a business that any idiot can run—because sooner or later, any idiot probably is going to run it.'

"The idea is not just to find cheap businesses, but to find good businesses! I learned that a cheap business can kill you, but a good business won't. I remember investing in a Spanish textile company that was selling below net cash. The stock was cheap, but the business was so lousy that the management team not only failed to keep it operating, but also lost all of its cash and assets. So sustainability and quality matter!"

Investing Made Simple

Proving his investment knowhow for another two years, in 1993, Paramés began managing Bestinver's first investment fund, Bestinfond, which focused primarily on Spanish stocks. In 2005, however, its investment mandate was changed to include international stocks. The rationale for the change was that local stocks provided little value at the time; hence to improve its flexibility, the fund began to look to surrounding markets.

Paramés explained his investment process: "First and foremost, I read a lot, and we never use investment screens to generate any ideas whatsoever. Our ideas come from reading newspapers, books, magazines, analysts' reports, and even our competitors' investment holdings. We also frequently brainstorm with people from different industries.

"It is important to know that idea generation comes from having a consistent understanding of the world and synchronizing it with all of the information you have accumulated. It is a disciplined process, and the sooner you begin this exercise, the more prepared you will be when opportunities arise. Ideas are not generated simply by waking up one day and saying, 'Let's look for an idea!' They require the accumulation of investment experience and the desire to learn over time!"

Deeply focused on investment research and analysis, Paramés rarely allows market noise to affect his well-being during the day. In fact, he does not check stock quotes until 6:00 P.M. each day. After all, he understands well enough from his reading of Benjamin Graham that the stock market is merely a platform for serving investors, not affecting their emotions.

Paramés stressed that when analyzing an investment, he does not use complicated financial models to evaluate it: "All I use is a simple calculator—to add, subtract, multiply, and divide. For example, we rarely use the discounted cash flow model[2] to calculate the value of a business unless it is a very stable one, such as a toll road or a utility company.

"I think it is not how sophisticated you are in your valuation model, but how well you know the business and how well you assess its competitive advantage. This cannot be modeled mathematically, but has more to do with the investor's own experience."

To determine competitive advantage, Paramés determines whether a business will still be around in ten years' time and whether its business model undergoes frequent change. If it fulfills these two prerequisites, then his evaluation process revolves around what makes the business special. For example, does it enjoy strong pricing power? Or does its industry have a high entry barrier to new threats? Although it is always ideal to speak to a business's management team, talking to its competitors, customers, former employees, and business suppliers is just as crucial.

Paramés explained: "Warren Buffett said that 'risk comes from not knowing what you're doing!' Reducing risk is not about adding assumptions and complicating your investment model, but about simplifying by investing in what you know best. If you believe that a business is sustainable, then you should think like an entrepreneur and try to calculate how much the business is worth, as if you were taking it over. If it is selling at a discount, then you have found value."

Believing that the fundamental concept of investing is to look for simple ideas, he concurs with Buffett, who once said: "I don't look to

---

[2] The discounted cash flow (DCF) model estimates the value of a business by projecting all of its future cash flows and then converting them into an equivalent present-day value.

jump over seven-foot bars. I look around for one-foot bars that I can step over!"

Paramés employs simple valuation multiples to evaluate his investments. He particularly likes to use the price-to-free-cash-flow ratio, which is a company's market capitalization divided by its free cash flow (FCF)—that is, the cash flow available for distribution to stakeholders. Found in the company's cash flow statement, FCF is operating cash flow minus capital expenditures.

He explained, "We like to buy good-quality businesses with FCF multiples of less than 11 to 12 times. Our target price is usually set at 15 times. The rationale for 15 is that it is the long-term average at which stocks generally trade. It also implies a FCF yield of around 6.6 percent—not too bad in most market environments.

"Of course, we always play around with the sensitivity of our assumptions to come up with a comfortable multiple. For example, if a business is good, then we use 17 times; if it is cyclical, then maybe 13 times."

Although this type of analysis sounds too simple to be true, it requires a prudent investor to come up with a reasonable estimate of the long-term FCF figure before assigning a fair multiple to it. Thus, applying such a method takes considerable skill and judgment.

The FCF method focuses on the valuation of a business. To determine its quality, Paramés employs return on capital employed (RoCE),[3] which measures the efficiency and profitability of its investments. In short, how well is the company deploying its capital?

Paramés believes that RoCE enables him to evaluate the quality of a business objectively. This metric gives him a good idea of the business's historical trends, and it also allows him to compare capital returns among different businesses.

He elaborated: "RoCE helps us to understand the competitive landscape of industries, from which we can try to determine the competitive advantages of different businesses. There is no ideal figure for RoCE. It is a moving number from quarter to quarter and from year to

---

[3] RoCE equals net operating profit after tax (NOPAT)/capital employed, where capital employed is total assets less current liabilities.

year, but we generally look for companies with consistent returns, and so we think around 20 percent is pretty good.

"The most important thing is to understand the business prospects. Even if RoCE looks good based on historical trends or in comparison with the business's competitors, it can still be a trap if the business does not have pricing power going forward. For example, if its profit margin is being squeezed by competition or inflation."

Austrian Economics and the Market

Legendary investor Philip Fisher wrote in *Common Stocks and Uncommon Profits*, "The amount of mental effort the financial community puts into this constant attempt to guess the economic future from a random and probably incomplete series of facts makes one wonder what might have been accomplished if only a fraction of such mental effort had been applied to something with a better chance of proving useful."

Echoing Fisher, Buffett once said, "Forecasts may tell you a great deal about the forecaster; they tell you nothing about the future."

Following Fisher's and Buffett's principles, Paramés has never been too concerned with the market consensus. This does not imply that he disregards macroeconomic figures. He follows such figures as gross domestic product growth, unemployment rates, and inflation rates to track the growth and stability of different markets. After all, the growth of a business is always affected by the growth of the economy in which it operates.

He explained, "I don't focus on the consensus opinion about a company or the economy because everyone has his or her own reality. My objective in life is to find my own truth and reality, both professionally and personally. There are too many forecasters, and they can be right for the wrong reasons or wrong for the right reasons. To remain focused, I have adopted Austrian economics as my investment framework."

Paramés was introduced to Austrian economics in 1997 when he began studying the philosophy of Ludwig von Mises and Friedrich Hayek. Unlike mainstream macroeconomic models, such as the Keynesian model or the Chicago School model, which involve a more mathematical way of analyzing the economy, the Austrian model has more to do with the observation of human action, also known as praxeology, the objective of which is to understand how different individuals affect economic phenomena.

"Mainstream economics focuses on empirical data, which leads economists into analyzing data and forecasting them. Because this exercise appears to be more scientific, politicians can use it to propose solutions to improve the economy," Paramés explained.

"The Austrian School believes that human actions cannot be predicted and that everyone has his or her own agenda under different circumstances, and so there is no real solution to curing real economic situations. In the long term, however, human actions will be adjusted accordingly and bring the economy to a normalized state because people are by nature entrepreneurial."

Whereas mainstream economists believe in market equilibrium and perfect competition, with each individual theoretically the same and striving for the same goal, the Austrians believe the market to be full of flesh-and-blood decision makers, who compete in the economy spontaneously through trial and error. This means the market is always at disequilibrium because different individuals have different intents and are constantly changing their actions, whether due to human error, the discovery of new information, a revised strategy, or personal constraints.

To give a simple analogy, the mainstream believes that the market is perfect to the extent that finding a dollar bill in the street would be too good to be true. If it was really there, then it would have been picked up long ago. The Austrians, however, believe the market can be imperfect. Therefore, it is possible that there is indeed a dollar bill in the street, and one can profit from someone else's negligence because good deals do appear from time to time.

The Austrian intellectual framework applies similarly to investing, as Paramés further explained: "It helps me to visualize how businesses evolve and compete, and how to distinguish between price and value in times of economic boom and bust.

"Because human behavior changes constantly, good businesses that became overvalued and bad businesses that became undervalued will eventually revert to their mean because every businessperson, in the spirit of an entrepreneur, will play his or her part in creating and destroying value. As equilibrium is hard to reach, businesses either overshoot or undershoot. For the investor, this framework suggests that value investing works, because with the right analysis, one can find good stocks that trade at discounts, and with patience, these stocks will eventually revert to their true worth."

Paramés stressed that this discussion only scratches the surface of Austrian economics. For a better understanding of this school of thought, he recommends reading *The Austrian School: Market Order and Entrepreneurial Creativity* by Spanish professor Jesús Huerta de Soto.

Reviewing his investment career, Paramés mentioned that Austrian economics also gave him a sense of reassurance in the midst of market frenzies: "I was getting worried in 1998 because stocks were becoming pricey. The Spanish stock market was up 39 percent in 1996, then 42 percent in 1997, and another 38 percent in 1998. With interest rates coming down from over 10 to 4 percent between 1995 and 1998, stocks had reasons to rally, but their valuations became quite unreasonable at one point."

In the summer of 1998, Paramés began to hold cash and utility stocks to defend his investment positions. His reading of Austrian economics suggested that a sustained period of low interest rates and credit creation would stimulate borrowing and growth in the economy, but when credit expansion became too excessive, human actions would naturally tend toward the extreme, thus creating a bubble and then a bust.

"I was convinced that a bubble was forming, and I was unwilling to compromise," Paramés said. "Clients were calling to complain that I wasn't taking advantage of the bull market, and those phone calls reached the point that I would have been more than happy to return their money and close down the business. I would rather have walked away than do something I wasn't comfortable with."

The stock market "fiesta" continued. With Internet stocks joining the party, every investor became a market genius. The Spanish market was up by 16 percent in 1999, but Paramés's Bestinfond was down by 11 percent.

This was a difficult moment for Paramés, but, in his darkest hour, he read an encouraging letter by Warren Buffett, who shared his view. In his 2000 annual report, Buffett wrote:

Nothing sedates rationality like large doses of effortless money. After a heady experience of that kind [the Internet bubble],

normally sensible people drift into behavior akin to that of
Cinderella at the ball. They know that overstaying the festiv-
ities . . . will eventually bring on pumpkins and mice. But they
nevertheless hate to miss a single minute of what is one helluva
party. Therefore, the giddy participants all plan to leave just
seconds before midnight. There's a problem, though: They are
dancing in a room in which the clocks have no hands.

Indeed, stocks that defied logic did eventually turn into pumpkins
and mice. In 2000, when the Spanish market tumbled 13 percent,
Bestinfond was up 13 percent. In 2001, when the market was down
another 6 percent, the fund was up 20 percent.

In 2006, Paramés sent a letter to Buffett to thank him for his
encouraging words, noting that being the only Spaniard who kept
his head when others were losing theirs was no easy task in the grip of
market mania. Buffett replied with a hand-written note asking Paramés
for investment ideas in Spain.

Although thrilled to be in touch with Buffett, Paramés remained
true to himself. He believed that Spain was about to go through tough
times due to the country's credit expansion in previous years. The end
result would be a collapse in the local real estate market, severely
affecting the Spanish economy as a whole. It was better to stay out of
Spain for the time being.

With skepticism and foresight, Paramés had sought investors' consent
to change Bestinfond's investment mandate to include foreign stocks in
the portfolio as early as 2005. Diversification away from Iberian stocks
was the only rational way to brace for the coming crisis.

Although not directly related to his investment career, a plane crash
in March 2006 had a profound effect on Paramés. Flying to Pamplona in
the north of Spain to attend an investor meeting, the plane in which he
was traveling hit the side of a mountain and crashed, killing Bestinver's
administration director and the copilot and severely injuring all of the
passengers onboard. Being the only person able to walk, Paramés
wandered the mountain for an hour searching for help. The accident
taught him that in life and in investing, mankind's ultimate essence is the
quest for survival.

A Global Rebalancing

For many investment funds around the world, "long term" is a luxury. Faced with constant pressure, fund managers are required to prove themselves in the shortest period of time to raise capital and retain investors.

Bestinver, in contrast, has a unique long-term culture that is fully supported by its parent company, Acciona, and its owners, who provide not only part of its capital, but also a pressure-free environment for Paramés to do what he does best.

He explained, "I think Bestinver's competitive advantage is that it has a very long-term investment approach. By that, I don't mean the next four to five years, but the next twenty to thirty years. Many long-term funds have a stock-holding period of four to give years, whereas we sometimes have a ten-year buying period for a stock. That's what we mean by long term!"

A one-man band, Paramés managed the Bestinfond and Bestinver Internacional funds by himself until 2003, when Álvaro Guzmán de Lázaro Mateos joined Bestinver as fund manager. In 2006, another fund manager, Fernando Bernad Marrase, also joined the team in its value hunt.

"With only Bestinfond, I basically had to cover around 100 Spanish stocks. All I did was to keep close track of them and then reshuffle or rebalance them based on their stock performance," Paramés said.

"After launching Bestinver Internacional in 1997, there were roughly hundreds of foreign stocks to cover. There is a saying that for every x kilometers, you have to divide the quality of your assessment by half. With a growing list of stocks to cover, Álvaro and Fernando apply their expertise to dig deeper in our analysis to make better judgments on foreign stocks. We also hired a Taiwanese analyst recently who is now stationed in China. He brings local knowledge to our understanding of Asia."

Bestinver currently offers more than ten investment funds. With several mutual funds, pension funds, and a hedge fund, this may seem an overwhelming workload for any investment manager, but Paramés clarified, "Technically, we only have two portfolios: a global portfolio and an Iberian portfolio. All of our funds are really combinations of these two. What we do is blend the allocation of stocks from our two port-folios to fit the purpose of each fund. It is as if we are cocktail mixers with two ingredients, and yet we blend different drinks to suit clients' needs."

A typical value fund has a low portfolio turnover rate, which means the manager does not buy and sell stocks frequently. Bestinver's funds, in contrast, tend to have very high portfolio turnover rates—often more than 100 percent. Changes in individual stock names, however, are typically few, with a replacement rate of only 25 percent.

Paramés elaborated: "We quite frequently buy and sell our portfolio stocks, but the names of our stocks don't change! We may move a stock from a 2 percent weighting to 5 percent, and then move another holding from 7 to 4 percent. The thing is: When a stock has gone up 20 percent, it is 20 percent less attractive, and so we mix and match our stock weighting to create a comfortable balance for the portfolio.

"Unlike the U.S., which has a high capital gains tax, in Europe the capital gains tax is only 1 percent if you sell a stock within a fund. That gives us the advantage of being able to switch between stocks and rebalance them whenever we want. The real taxation comes at the fund level, and so I constantly tell our investors not to sell our funds, and to let us do the buying and selling of stocks. Fortunately, many of our investors are long-term driven, even passing the funds on to their children, and so they don't have to pay any taxes."

Under European Undertakings for Collective Investment in Transferable Securities (UCITS) rules, investment funds are not allowed to hold a concentrated portfolio of just a few stocks. Accordingly, Bestinver usually holds 50 stocks on average in its Iberian and interna-tional portfolios, with the top 10 holdings accounting for 40 to 50 percent of the portfolio.

Reviewing his career, Paramés said he believes that when an investment principle is sound, it is crucial to stick to it for the long haul and not compromise by following the world's fads and crazes: "Many people chase hot trends or find a short-term catalyst in an investment. What we care about most is simply whether or not a business is going in the right direction over the next ten years. If it is, then we patiently wait for it to realize its true value. We have some stocks that we have been holding for fifteen years."

After having been in the investment management business for twenty years, Paramés admits that he has been doing exactly the same thing all this time. Obviously, his long experience adds value to his judgments today, but his investment process has always remained the same.

He elaborated, "I don't think the investment landscape has changed much because human mentality is always the same. Every economic situation is different, but there are always similarities. The Austrian economics model explains this well. Whether the times are good or bad, I would say that the emotional quotient is more important than the intelligence quotient!"

Bestinver's success has made Paramés a value investing force in Spain. He has shown the Spanish investment community that a prudent investment manager can really add value to an investment portfolio. Although the fund management industry in Europe is dominated by the big banks, the business of which is oriented toward a sales and marketing agenda, Paramés has proved that an independent fund house can be honest and direct in its dealings.

Paramés and his team hold an investors' meeting every year, which he calls a "wedding party" because it provides an opportunity for fellow investors to mingle and share ideas with one another. Similar to the annual Berkshire Hathaway meeting hosted by Warren Buffett and Charlie Munger, the Bestinver annual meeting gives investors a chance to ask Paramés any questions they like. The gala event instills investors with confidence and preaches the importance of a long-term mindset and discipline.

Married in 1997, Paramés has two sons and three daughters. In addition to such family activities as vacations and visits to the beach, his main hobbies are watching basketball games and reading. As a father, he knows that setting a good example is the best way to teach his children. Value investing is similar. Indeed, although the value approach may never be trendy, at least a person will never go wrong by following its logic and principles.

Paramés concluded: "The greatest joy in investing is finding an investment that is undervalued. The happiness that affords really can't be explained! When I find such an investment, I often think it must be impossible. Then I look again and, if it's really true, I am as excited as if I have found a treasure. That joy and passion is what I want to convey to my children because the world is full of treasures. If you don't find them, then you can still enjoy the journey, but if you do, then you have discovered the value of life!"

CHAPTER 7

The Income-Conscious Englishman

Anthony Nutt
Jupiter Asset Management

A wise man will live as much within his wit as within his income.

—*Lord Chesterfield*

*J*upiter Asset Management is a U.K.-based asset management group that specializes in equity and bond investments for private and institutional investors. Established in 1985 as a specialist boutique, the company has since grown to become one of the largest and most successful British investment companies with £22.8 billion in assets under management.

As head of Jupiter's income and U.K. equities teams and director of Jupiter Asset Management Limited, Anthony Nutt currently manages four investment funds: the Jupiter Income Trust, Jupiter High Income Fund (Unit Trust), Jupiter Dividend and Growth Trust, and the equity portfolio of the Jupiter Distribution Fund.

Since joining the company in 1996, Nutt has outperformed the U.K. stock market consistently. For example, between the launch of the £506 million Jupiter High Income Trust in February 1996 and December 2011, Nutt generated 316.07 percent, or 9.38 percent per annum. During the same period, its benchmark index, the FTSE All-Share Index, grew 159.93 percent, or 6.19 percent annually.

Another notable fund that Nutt manages is the £2 billion Jupiter Income Trust. As of December 2011, he had generated 93.83 percent, or 5.83 percent annually, since taking over the fund on April 30, 2000. Its benchmark index, FTSE All-Share Index, grew 9.33 percent, or 2.88 percent per annum, during the same period.

Value investment funds are widely available in the United States, but in the United Kingdom, the word "value" is not as often used to describe an investment product. Instead, the British prefer the words "income" or "dividend."

Anthony Nutt said, "I presume the term 'value' is preferred in the U.S. because many legendary American investors have written books about the topic. In the U.K., value investing has actually been around for a long period of time, but we don't often say it because investing is all about seeking value in the first place, so it is unnecessary to add the word to an investment scheme.

"When looking for value investments, however, the British demand fund managers generate returns in the form of dividends or income. Be they conglomerates, consumer staples, or utility companies, British investors prefer a level of comfort through dividend payouts from companies because they are the only tangible proof of investment returns."

Nutt's life and career experiences may provide a hint or two that will help to explain Britain's investment culture.

Born in 1953 in the Midlands, Anthony Nutt would be classified as a baby boomer in the United States. At the time of his birth, Britain was in a period of recovery following what Sir Winston Churchill called a period of "blood, sweat and tears."

Nutt recalled that people were extremely frugal in the 1950s with the rationing from World War II continuing. People added only a few items of comfort to their homes and led very modest lifestyles. The country had once pushed for peace and prosperity, only to see itself devastated by the European conflict. The experience taught people to look for tangible returns rather than bet on rosy assumptions.

"While growing up, I didn't have any dreams except I wished to work in the City [London] one day," said Nutt. "In the mid-1960s, there was a movement toward distance learning and night classes, and it became apparent that you could get a university degree whilst working. I was interested in the program so I enrolled at the Open University to study a wide range of subjects, including philosophy, politics, and economics."

Working and studying in the early 1970s, Nutt was well aware of the uncertainty of the British economy. As high rates of inflation prompted the government to cap wage growth in the public sector, trade unions went on strike. Industrial action by coal miners, in particular, led to power outages across the country.

The Conservative government of the day responded to the crisis by introducing the Three-Day Week to reduce electricity consumption. In effect, working hours were shortened, and lights were switched off at a certain hour.

Nutt recalled, "I was living in Earls Court in London, and the city became very quiet after dark. In addition to the Three-Day Week, there was an oil crisis in 1973, quickly followed by a string of bank collapses. NatWest Bank almost went bust, and the government had to inject liquidity into the financial system to rescue the economy. It was a difficult and transitional moment for the British people, including myself."

Aside from school, Nutt worked with the Ministry of Defence (MoD) in the Procurement Executive. His duties involved overseeing the sale and purchase of arms. "I must say it was an interesting time to be working for the MoD," Nutt said. "However, the job was not particularly rewarding in terms of rapid progress or other attractions except that I was allowed to continue working in the City."

After a little more than two years as a civil servant, Nutt decided to move into stockbroking, joining Foster & Braithwaite, a well-known U.K. brokerage firm, although he remained there for only a short time. He explained, "I worked in stockbroking for a total of eight years. In those years I took a lot of qualification exams and learned about financial statement analysis and investment research.

"One day, I came to the conclusion that I wanted to manage money for a living. Since stockbroking is on the sell side—giving investment advice and executing trades for clients—I ultimately had to be on the buy side in order to manage money. Finding a job offering as assistant to a fund manager, I left stockbroking for good and joined the fund management industry."

A Victorian Mindset

After switching to the buy side in the early 1980s, Nutt initially worked at Family Assurance, an organization that manages money on behalf of what are known as friendly societies.

"Before there were insurance and welfare, people came together to form friendly societies so they could achieve common financial and social goals," Nutt explained. "The friendly society concept is a very old Victorian concept which encouraged people to contribute their savings to the society regularly, and then, over a fixed period of time, they would receive a fixed return."

Regular savings, spending below one's means, and living modestly were traditional values in Victorian Britain. Indeed, Charles Dickens advised the readers of *David Copperfield*: "Annual income twenty pounds, annual expenditure nineteen six, result happiness. Annual income twenty pounds, annual expenditure twenty pound ought and six, result misery."

At Family Assurance, Nutt was delegated the tasks of analyzing stocks and looking for companies that paid dividends. After a while, he came to realize that an emphasis on dividend yields alone was a mistake. More crucial were the prospects and valuation of the business. Gradually, he became value conscious in his investment analysis.

Nutt commented, "You cannot compare dividend yields across companies and make a simple investment case out of it. You have to analyze the prospects of businesses and see if they can grow their dividends over time. With growing dividends, you get growing income, which effectively allows you to reinvest your capital so that you can have compounding effects for your investments."

"Since the stock market can be fanatical, business valuation is also important because better returns tend to be made with lower valuations and over a longer period of time. From what I do now at Jupiter and even from my days as a stockbroker, I observed that in the U.K., if you buy a stock at 30 times earnings, historical and empirical evidence have shown that over time its investment return will be more modest than if you buy a stock with only 5 times earnings."

With considerable fund management experience under his belt, Nutt took on greater responsibilities and joined U.K. Provident in 1984. Just two years later, he moved to the Trustee Savings Bank (TSB) and became the official fund manager of the bank's £1.5 billion General Unit Trust.

Managing one of the largest investment trusts in the United Kingdom, Nutt faced his first challenge as a professional fund manager: "My challenge was not the size of the fund, but rather I had to spend a tremendous amount of effort and time to sort out stock holdings in the portfolio that was handed over to me."

Nutt explained that the small-cap boom of the 1980s had led the fund's previous manager to invest heavily in small companies. The origins of the small-cap boom dated back to the 1970s, when the British economy was in difficulty and many businesses went bust. As the economy began to recover in the 1980s, small companies with high growth prospects began to emerge. As they went public, they not only gave strong momentum to the stock market, but also led to a period of multiple expansion, as investors were eager to pay for higher-than-average P/E multiples.

At the same time, large conglomerates were also contributing to the stock market rally, regularly making headlines for their purchases of smaller companies to maintain a high rate of growth. Nutt explained: "U.K. conglomerates were going around the world and buying up businesses. They rationalized them, cost cut them, and improved their bottom line. Because these conglomerates were successful in buying companies, their high valuation was reflected in their stock price. And because of that, it became a self-generating investment model. They would continue to takeover lowly valued businesses and add earnings to their income statements."

"Obviously, that model lost its charm after a while and investors lost faith in it. After October 1987, investors finally recognized that these conglomerates were playing an accounting game by maintaining their own high multiples by buying low-multiples companies to increase earnings. With write-offs, write-backs, and 'one-time' accounting adjustments, investors finally recognized that conglomerates weren't value plays at all. They were more of an operation based on accounting models and financial gearing."

After taking over the fund at TSB, Nutt decided he wanted value stocks in the portfolio, rather than momentum or multiple expansion stocks, so he decided to cut down his positions in small-cap companies and other holdings. This decision proved to be a very sensible one indeed, not to mention timely, with the Black Monday crash occurring on October 19, 1987.

Nutt recalled, "In July 1987, the U.K. index topped out and over the summer it had a lot of volatility. While I was already skeptical about the market, my conviction to sell was further confirmed after listening to

Financial World Tonight, which was a very popular financial radio program in the U.K. Those interviewed on the program were starting to give poor investment tips and recommend speculative ideas, and it became apparent to me that there wasn't a great deal of value in the market.

"With the market becoming a bit gung ho and stocks all priced according to blue sky scenarios, I not only tried to sell down on small-cap stocks, but I literally tried to sell down on stocks to raise cash. On the Wednesday before Black Monday, I managed to raise £200 million by selling our positions through a program trade. Then, on the Friday, we had the biggest storm ever in the country. No one could get to work, and the stock market was closed. Then Monday came and the market tumbled."

The TSB fund was fortunate to be highly liquid at the time, Nutt explained, and was able to buy a number of undervalued stocks after the crash. "Black Monday really gave me confirmation that value investing works," he added. "It not only works for buying undervalued stocks, but also for selling overvalued ones before trouble happens."

Stock valuations changed after 1987. The small-cap frenzy began to wane, conglomerates began to fall out of favor, P/E multiples reverted to their mean, and the Victorian concept of steady income gradually regained favor. As Charles Dickens put it, "There is nothing so strong or safe in an emergency of life as the simple truth!"

Focusing purely on the quality of businesses and their valuation, Nutt took the General Unit Trust to the next level, and the fund began consistently to outperform its peers.

Finding the Right Investment Culture

Looking back at Black Monday and its aftermath, Nutt pointed out that the general investment landscape in the United Kingdom remained positive. Retail savings continued to power ahead as the Thatcher administration promoted investments through various programs, such as the Personal Equity Plans (PEPs). The PEPs program, introduced in 1986, relieved investors of income and capital gains tax up to certain annual limits.

On top of PEPs, the government pushed for the privatization of state-owned enterprises throughout the 1980s, which encouraged every British citizen to participate in the stock market.

"If you look at the British market, it was generally bullish from the early 1980s to the late 1990s," Nutt said. "For example, from 1982 to 1998, the FTSE Index had an annualized return of roughly 13 to 14 percent. After Black Monday, the index took about two years to recover, but since then it had continued to reach new heights."

Thanks to his stellar performance at TSB, Nutt was approached by Fleming Investment Management in 1989. After managing that firm's £2 billion fund for several years, Nutt joined Jupiter Asset Management in 1996, where he remains.

Having now been in the fund management business for more than 30 years, Nutt believes that to produce a sustainable investment record over the long term, a value fund manager has to find an investment workplace that shares his or her value investing mindset.

He explained, "You can't get away from the fact that the stock market is a casino in the short term. As it is a common paradox that long-term returns are achieved by short-term targets, you can't deny that many investment companies constantly aim for short-term results. I don't like to treat the market like a casino, so I'd rather focus on the long term and have a buy-and-hold strategy. At the same time, it is important to find the right investment company that thinks the way you do.

"When it comes to value investing, my investment team and I believe that the difficult part lies not in finding out whether a stock is cheap or dear. We can always look at a business objectively and come up with a fair opinion about it. The more difficult part is that we never know if other investors are identifying the very same stock and thinking the same thing as us. In essence, determining how long it takes for an undervalued stock to perform is totally out of our control.

"Because of that, we never have a time horizon for our investments. We focus purely on valuation instead. Sometimes we exit an investment when its business has become fully matured or its business return begins to deteriorate. Sometimes we hold on to an investment for years because its value remains attractive. Investment exit, then, is never a timing exercise, but a valuation one."

Nutt cited the example of the technology, media, and telecoms (TMT) boom in the late 1990s, a period of excessive valuation during which a number of traditional stocks were trading at only 4 to 5 times P/E ratios: "No one was interested in those old-economy stocks because investors thought the Internet was going to replace them. Although we had no idea when investors would become interested in those stocks again, we continued to hold them as they provided good returns. When the TMT boom turned to a bust, investors finally recognized how low the valuations of our stocks were."

Nutt and Jupiter Fund Management's shared investment philosophy allows them to think for the long term and generate investment returns in a non-fanatic way.

Launched in 1985, Jupiter was at first a specialist investment boutique. Over the years, it has fostered a culture that allows an entrepreneurial spirit. Fund managers are discouraged from being closet index trackers who passively mimic the returns of the stock market. Instead, they are encouraged to invest freely as long as the investment in question fits their fund's objectives.

Without an in-house stock list or market view, individual fund managers have the freedom to make decisions independently. After all, Jupiter insists that "a committee-based approach can lead people into a rather weak compromise that ends in mediocre performance." Based on its fundamental and bottom-up approach to stock picking, the company asks only that its managers "optimize performance over the medium to long term without exposing investors to unnecessary risk."

Nutt added, "When I joined Jupiter, it was emerging as one of the more successful retail investment houses in the country because its charismatic founders had established the right culture and business pace. Within just a few weeks of joining the company, I became responsible for the launch of the Jupiter High Income Trust. Whether you call it income investing or value investing, the underlying concept of the fund is to seek low-valuation stocks that provide an upside and ensure the safety of investments."

Trusting Only Tangible Income

When attempting to identify investments, Nutt looks for undervalued businesses with a strong and sustainable cash flow. At the same time, he makes sure that these businesses have a standing commitment to distribute income in the form of dividends, special dividends, or share buybacks.

Nutt explained, "The British culture encourages me to look for tangible returns rather than bet on blue sky scenarios. If you look at dividends alone, the U.K. leads the world in terms of high dividend payout ratios.

"I have seen many businesses that promise growth, but instead of distributing income to shareholders, they bet on a multiple expansion model. When the market falls out of love with this sentiment-driven scheme, these businesses have nothing tangible to offer shareholders.

"To find the right investment, you must look for businesses that generate sufficient return on capital and sustainable cash flow so that investors can be rewarded for their investment. In effect, paying dividends is a way to convince investors to remain invested in the business."

As an example, Nutt cited a hypothetical opportunity to invest in a gold mine: "You naturally expect to generate returns on your investment, so you give management the capital to develop the business, then you expect them to monetize the gold mine and allocate resources accordingly. As management set aside capital for expenditures and business development, you also expect them to pay you back your invested capital. I think this is a very logical framework for doing business, but the problem is that many investors are never paid back because management often bets on the stock market to do the job for them by pushing their stock price higher."

While taking a bottom-up, pragmatic approach to value investing, Nutt cautioned that looking purely at the numbers can be misleading.

He explained, "We don't just look at the numbers or yields alone to make an investment decision. Although we analyze dividend yields, payout ratios, P/E multiples, return on invested capital, and free cash flow, we believe that looking at these numbers is too simplistic. While I subscribe to the idea that all roads lead to Rome, and whatever criteria you use to value a stock ultimately gives you an idea of what's cheap or dear, the more important aspect is qualitative analysis.

"Most of our analysis focuses on understanding businesses and their strategic intent. We spend each year looking at over 500 companies, and we get in touch with each company two to three times a year."

To determine strategic intent, Nutt talks to companies' management teams and tries to understand their goals and aspirations for the business, and he applies Michael Porter's five forces to his analysis: threat of new competition, threat of substitute products or services, bargaining power of customers (buyers), bargaining power of suppliers, and intensity of competitive rivalry.

Nutt elaborated: "We try to assess to what degree a business is plausible. Will it be able to execute its business model successfully? Is its management capable? If the business is good, can it grow its dividends over time? These are some of the questions we ask.

"Sometimes I am uncomfortable analyzing a business that targets high growth, but at the same time we need growth in a business to ensure that it not only has the capability to pay dividends to investors, but also the capacity to grow those dividends over time. Whether or not there is growth, the key is to make sure that the valuation of the business isn't excessive and that you are not overpaying for growth."

Many value investors like to invest in companies with no debt. For Nutt, however, debt is something of a distraction. It is not an unpardonable sin as long as it serves a good purpose: "I like to see efficient balance sheets rather than worry if a company has debt or no debt because every situation is different. I've seen companies with cash-rich balance sheets, yet their business is poor. I've seen companies with high debt, yet their balance sheets are efficient.

"I think it is acceptable to have modest debt at a reasonable cost. As long as a company's management shows the strategic intent for it and proves that it can enhance shareholder value, then I support it."

At Jupiter, Nutt holds 100 to 110 stocks in each of his four managed funds, with the top 10 holdings usually making up 40 percent of each portfolio. Always taking a long-term approach, a strategic shift to any sector weighting tends to be gradual. Because of the size of the funds, entering and exiting investment positions can take weeks, if not months. Investors sometimes blame Nutt for buying too early or selling too soon, but in the main they understand the difficulty of maneuvering investment positions that are large in size.

As previously noted, Nutt is a bottom-up stock picker. Although the fundamentals of a business are most critical in stock picks, he acknowledges the implications of macroeconomic factors.

He said, "I believe that micro-, or bottom-up, analysis is always the main contributor to excess returns over time, but there is no doubt that macroeconomic policies have had great impacts on global stock markets over the past few years. By looking at these policies with a top-down view, my job is also to identify long-term business trends. Through picking the right sector, we think that good companies with varying degrees of success can do well in different economic cycles."

When everyone else was throwing themselves into Internet stocks, Nutt stayed well away, instead investing in the mining sector because its long-term prospects appeared favorable. After considering the implications of the Internet for traditional businesses, he concluded that the world still needs food to eat and oil to power the economy.

He explained, "We always look at the long-term impact of businesses. I still remember going to an analyst meeting at mining company Rio Tinto in 2000, and the CEO said that the demand for the company's products in China was something they had never experienced before. That was an important signal about the mining sector, but investors preferred to stay with Internet stocks. When Internet stocks went bust and investors began to invest in the mining sector in the mid-2000s, the story was not new to us."

In 2007, however, Nutt decided to sell all of his positions in mining because the sector's businesses had begun to deteriorate and their valuation had become too rich: "Mining companies had a model of returning cash to shareholders in the 1990s and early 2000s, but when the sector became too hot, managements were reluctant to distribute capital to shareholders and decided to expand their businesses. By 2007, some of them almost went bust because of over-expansion. We sold some mining shares at the top of the cycle because they no longer delivered shareholder value.

"At the same time, we began to buy pharmaceutical companies because after staying out from the sector for more than a decade, they were finally delivering shareholder value with reasonable valuations and sustainable dividend yields and growth. We got into the sector too early and were criticized by some investors, but over the past few years pharmaceutical stocks have delivered good income for our funds, and their share prices have also performed well.

"All in all, I think the hardest thing for companies to do is to allocate capital efficiently. As investors, our job is to analyze how efficiently they employ capital expenditure and how efficiently they return capital to shareholders. Then we try to determine their optimum debt level and fair value for the equity portion."

His observations of the market have led Nutt to conclude that one of the pitfalls in business today is over-reliance on management consultants or investment bankers, who are trying to take the lead role in traditional businesses. Because these professionals attempt to build businesses by focusing on financial gearing and short-term results to impress investors, they tend to lose sight of the long term and of real business value.

Nutt commented, "When you move people from investment banking roles to nuts-and-bolts-type companies, they tend to be conceited and do things that are more exotic. I am very weary of these personalities because the market always cheers them on for their turnaround capability in the short term, only to notice later that they have destroyed shareholder value and damaged the long-term prospects of a once respectable business."

The Courage to Keep Going

Sir Winston Churchill once said that "success is not final, failure is not fatal: it is the courage to continue that counts!"

Looking back over his investment career, Nutt said that he has enjoyed every moment of his time in fund management. Whether his investment funds are having an up or down year, he never worries too much because his focus on value and dividends means that any short-term market volatility is safeguarded by periodic income. Then, as volatility evens out over the longer term, investments begin to emerge with good value.

Nutt said, "2007 to 2008 was tough because some of our media investments were poor. The sector was not as robust as we had expected. That said, I think I haven't had a period when I felt awful about my investment decisions because as a fund manager you need to have confidence in your decisions and avoid self-doubt. If you have doubts that become too overwhelming, and you can't take the challenge, then you shouldn't be in fund management in the first place.

"After all, seeking value is an enjoyable job because you go along with different companies, and as they progress, your investments progress. By focusing on the long term, you can go through economic cycles without worrying about long or short, black or white. You just keep going and see how your own investments perform."

Nutt recently read an article citing a poll in which fund managers were asked whom they would choose to run their own money. Most gave the same answer: myself. Nutt commented, "Forgive me if I sound a little pompous, but I absolutely feel the same because I am confident in my ability. I feel that successful investing has much more to do with individual thinking than general consensus. As long as you have the right temperament and time horizon for your investments, I think you can trust your own judgment rather than others."

The U.S. financial crisis in 2008 and the ongoing European sovereign debt crisis since 2010 have led Nutt to believe that the developed world will be somewhat static for the foreseeable future, growing modestly and moderately: "What concerns me most is a potential compression of investment valuation. There will be fewer anomalies at the high end and low end in the stock universe, so value investors will have arguably less opportunity to make money out of deep value stocks in a way that's been done in the last thirty to forty years.

"We are now also in a world where the rich and well-off have more than they need, so it is a vice to have conspicuous consumption and instant gratification. In that respect, I tend to stay away from the retail sector as I believe the world should return to a savings economy from the current spending one. In fact, I tell my kids to focus on value and never overspend."

A keen cyclist and father of two sons and two daughters, Nutt tries to instill the value mindset in his family members. Investing, like cycling, is both an individual game on the micro level and a team exercise on the macro level. He concluded, "I am a frequent spectator of the Tour de France. One thing I have learned from cycling, which is also true of investing, is that whether you lead or you fall behind, it doesn't matter. It's all about having the endurance to finish the race and the courage to continue!"

CHAPTER 8

The Frequent Value Traveler

Mark Mobius
Templeton Emerging Markets Group

Two roads diverged in a wood, and I—I took the one less traveled by, and that has made all the difference.

—*Robert Frost*

*M*ark Mobius is the executive chairman of Templeton Emerging Markets Group, a subsidiary of Franklin Templeton Investments. Currently managing the group's emerging market portfolios and overseeing an investment team that spans 17 market locations in Asia, Latin America, Africa, and Eastern Europe, Mobius was handpicked by global investing pioneer and billionaire Sir John Templeton in 1987 to manage the first emerging markets fund listed on the New York Stock Exchange, the Templeton Emerging Markets Fund.

Starting with initial capital of $100 million, Mobius and his team have grown Templeton emerging markets funds into a business worth more than $50 billion (as of the end of 2011). From its inception on July 31, 1989, to December 31, 2011, its flagship investment trust, the Templeton Emerging Markets Investment Trust, generated 2,071.5 percent, or 14.72 percent annually. During the same period, its benchmark index, the MSCI Emerging Markets Index, returned 866.4 percent, or 10.65 percent per annum.

Often dubbed the "dean of emerging markets" or, more affectionately, the "Yul Brynner of Wall Street," thanks to his signature bald appearance, Mobius was one of Asiamoney's "Top 100 Most Powerful and Influential People" in 2006.

The magazine's editors wrote that Mobius "boasts one of the highest profiles of any investor in the region and is regarded by many in the financial industry as *one of the most successful emerging markets investors over the last 20 years. Despite tough times during the financial crisis nine years ago, he still commands a strong following in the investment world and is influencing the direction of billions of investment dollars."*

After earning bachelor's and master's degrees from Boston University, Mobius obtained a PhD in economics and political science from the Massachusetts Institute of Technology (MIT). He is the author of 11 books, including Trading with China, The Investors' Guide to Emerging Markets, Mobius on Emerging Markets, Passport to Profits, Equities—An Introduction to the Core Concepts, Mutual Funds—An Introduction to the Core Concepts, and Foreign Exchange—An Introduction to the Core Concepts.

Mark Mobius first became familiar with the stock market in 1973. While running Mobius Inc., a Hong Kong–based business consulting company, he was asked by a wealthy local client to conduct research on the stock market. As he had little investment knowledge, he reviewed market charts and applied technical analysis to his research.

Mobius recalled, "At that time I had not learned about fundamental stock analysis. I picked up a book on technical analysis and I started analyzing the Hong Kong stock market movements. Having studied psychology, I liked the idea of technical analysis since it seemed to take psychology and particularly social psychology into account.

"Looking at market charts was also somewhat similar to conducting consumer surveys, which was my main job in the consulting business. My research led me to the conclusion that a very common chart pattern was forming—the head and shoulders formation.[1] Knowing that the stock market was red hot at the time and that its chart pattern signaled a trend reversal, I advised my client to stay away from stocks."

The Hong Kong stock market did drop shortly thereafter and did not recover for many years. Before the tumble, however, Mobius failed

---

[1] The head and shoulders chart formation signals a price reversal from either a bullish or bearish trend.

to follow his own advice and put money into a stock called Mosbert Holdings.

Mosbert Holdings was a Malaysia-based, Hong Kong–listed holding company. Although the company's background was mysterious and no one had any idea where its money came from, it kept making noise in the region by regularly acquiring companies and properties. When the company's stock dropped from HK$8.0 to HK$3.5, a colleague recommended it to Mobius, and they both decided to take advantage of the beaten-down investment opportunity. As it turned out, Mosbert was a scam, and the company soon collapsed.

Mobius confessed, "I tried to do some due diligence by calling up the company to get some information, but the person who answered was unfriendly and said nothing was available in print. He even hung up on me! Going against my better judgment, I listened to my friend, who assured me that the company was to become Asia's next financial miracle.

"What I learned from this mistake was never to take other people's advice when making an investment decision! Always make decisions based on what you have learned and act on the information that you have gathered. Even if you turn out to be wrong, at least you can learn from your own mistakes."

Another lesson that Mobius learned from the experience is that although technical analysis can be useful, fundamental analysis is more important because it is the only way to find out what a company is actually worth. In the case of Mosbert, the lack of available information should have told him to stay well away from it: "I became a firm believer in getting out there and kicking the tires, and so fundamental analysis has become my primary focus. At Templeton, our investment team does look at stock charts, but we never make an investment decision without fundamental research on the company's financials, management, and industry dynamics."

After carrying out more research on the stock market in the early 1970s, Mobius became increasingly interested in finance, and so he joined international securities firm Vickers Da Costa in 1980 to conduct studies of financial markets in Asia. This was something of a career shift as he was a business and marketing consultant by training.

Reading between the Minds

Born in 1936 in Hempstead, New York, Joseph Bernhard Mark Mobius is the son of German and Puerto Rican parents.

He reminisced, "When I was a kid, I first wanted to be a doctor, then I wanted to be in government service, and later on I decided I wanted to be an entertainer, either an actor or a pianist. In fact, when we were in high school, my brothers and I formed a trio, with me on piano and my brothers playing the violin and cello. In college, I played the piano in bars at night for fun, and the money helped to subsidize my education."

Mobius received a scholarship to study fine arts at Boston University in 1955. Although the subject may seem somewhat irrelevant to a business career, it indirectly stimulated his interest in exploring the world. He explained, "Studying fine arts gave me a broad perspective on the human experience and our civilization. As I learned more about different cultures and how different people perceive the world, I became interested in communications and human psychology."

After earning a bachelor's degree in 1958, Mobius decided to stay on at Boston University to further his education in communications, receiving his master's in 1959. His great thirst for knowledge not yet slaked, he then enrolled in the University of Wisconsin to study political science and social psychology, where he had an opportunity to take part in an exchange program to study abroad in Japan. Excited about the chance to travel to the Far East, Mobius embarked on a crash course in Japanese history and language before heading off.

"At the Institute of Humanistic Studies at Kyoto University, I learned about mass communications in Japan," he said. "Because it was not too long after the Second World War, propaganda analysis was still quite the vogue in academic circles, and so I decided to specialize in it. While studying, I also worked at Asahi Broadcasting Corp., where I researched the Japanese consumer market and sold broadcast time to American advertisers."

Returning to the United States in 1961, Mobius studied experimental psychology and served as a teaching assistant at the University of New Mexico. During summer vacation, he also joined the advertising firm BBDO as a research analyst to process consumer survey data and analyze consumer and mass market behavior.

Mobius's consumer data research alerted him to the booming economic development in different parts of the world. To learn more about economics, he enrolled at MIT to pursue a doctorate. At the same time, he also served as a research assistant there, analyzing survey data to reveal the characteristics of educational TV viewers. In 1964, Mobius received his PhD.

Having achieved the highest academic qualification and having enjoyed his time in Japan, Mobius decided to move to Asia. Equipped with extensive knowledge of communications and psychology, his goal was to find a post that would allow him to connect businesses in the East and West. He joined International Research Associates in Tokyo as a consulting research coordinator, where his focus was on understanding consumer behavior in the region.

Over the next few years, Mobius conducted thousands of interviews and analyzed more than 100 consumer brands from around the world. This opportunity not only afforded him knowledge of different types of businesses but also helped him gain in-depth insight into what would and would not work in the Asian business environment.

For example, on one assignment, he was sent to Hong Kong to do consultancy work for Monsanto, a multinational agricultural biotechnology corporation, on the feasibility of distributing a new high-protein drink in Asia. Before he could advise the firm, he first had to understand consumer behavior and soft drink consumption in Asia, and then he had to analyze the production capability and distribution logistics of the area. Although his work could be seen solely as marketing research, it required Mobius to truly understand the value chain of the business before drawing a conclusion.

He noted, "My consumer research experience provided a good background for what I do now because it involved social psychology, which ultimately affects business sentiment and the economy. It also taught me how to tackle and research an idea. Although I had no intention of becoming an investment fund manager at the time, my job gave me the confidence to analyze businesses and eventually to start my own firm."

After the Monsanto project, the company offered him a job at the head office in St. Louis, Missouri, but Mobius decided to stay in Hong Kong, as he had grown fond of the city. His experience dealing with

Asians of different cultures and developing the know-how to connect Eastern and Western businesses gave him the confidence to found Mobius Inc., a research-oriented business consulting firm in 1969.

Thinking Big and Small

Starting out with a small team of local Chinese staff, Mobius Inc. began to connect the dots. The company helped a Swiss pharmaceutical company set up a sales operation in Taiwan, assisted an American exporter in selling toilet soap additives in Indonesia, and conducted feasibility studies for a multinational dairy producer to determine whether a particular type of cheese was suitable for the Japanese market.

Now his own boss, Mobius had to learn the art of consulting big businesses and running a small one. He recalled, "I was providing local intelligence to foreign companies to do big business in Asia, but had no idea how to run my own firm!

"I was constantly flying around Asia, and my revenues simply didn't cover my expenses. To make matters worse, I put in low-ball bids for projects that wouldn't even cover my costs. Learning from my local staff, I eventually found bucket shops where I could buy discounted airline tickets, and instead of dining out, we ordered lunch boxes and ate in the office.

"Over time, I became frugal and value conscious, and I came to realize that saving money can be more prestigious than making money. Becoming partly Chinese in spirit, I started focusing more on the numbers and being more conservative. I wouldn't say the firm became a cash cow over the next ten years, but it became a stable business operation."

Mobius's experience in Asia also inspired him to write a book in 1973. In *Trading with China*, he discusses the dos and don'ts of the Chinese marketplace. To spread the gospel further, he became a guest lecturer in marketing, social psychology, and consumer psychology at Hong Kong University and the Chinese University of Hong Kong.

In the early 1970s, Mobius and his team found their niche in industrial market research. While building their Asian networks, they often came across unique business propositions. On one occasion they were offered the chance to distribute stuffed Snoopy dogs.

Mobius explained, "One day, a woman from San Francisco named Connie Boucher walked into our office. She asked if we could find her a manufacturer to produce Snoopy dogs, for which she had a license from Snoopy's creator, Charles Schulz. I helped her out getting production going in Asia. When I saw how well her products were selling in the U.S., I asked whether she had ever considered selling them in Asia. She said, 'Why don't you do it?' So we began distributing Snoopy dogs. Eventually, the toy business became bigger than our research business, and as my personal interest was in research, I sold the toy operation to my Chinese staff."

There were two elements to Mobius's affinity with Snoopy. The beloved cartoon character made him a considerable amount of money, but a small accident involving the dog's stuffed incarnation also led to a more personal decision.

Mobius explained: "Snoopy dogs were overrunning our office, so I asked my staff to store some of them at my place while I was away in South Korea. On my return, I was awakened in the middle of the night by a strange smell, which turned out to be burning Snoopy dogs, as they had been placed near a heating coil. I managed to put out the fire, but not before my bright red hair was singed. As I'd already lost half of it, I decided to shave off the rest, and ever since I've quite enjoyed my new hairstyle."

A Chinese saying has it that "of every ten bald men, nine are rich." As Hong Kong was quickly becoming an international trading and financial hub in the 1970s, with Mobius's business intelligence and new bald head, he was well placed to prove the saying true when he spotted an opportunity to provide clients with investment consultations.

After analyzing the Hong Kong stock market for the aforementioned client in 1973 and having learned from his investment mistake with Mosbert Holdings, Mobius realized that in-depth research into companies' financials and management capabilities is key. Equipped with a thrifty mindset from running his own firm, the soon-to-be "dean of emerging markets" gradually transformed himself into a value-oriented investor.

In 1980, Mobius decided to sell his consulting business and analyze investments full time. He joined international securities firm Vickers Da Costa as a securities analyst. Primarily investigating the securities markets of Hong Kong and the Philippines, Mobius also carried out extensive research on the high-tech sector in Singapore, the oil sector in China, and blue chip companies in Taiwan. In 1983, he moved to Taiwan to help set up Vickers's Taiwan office and became responsible for the research and development of emerging securities markets, including Korea, Taiwan, the Philippines, Thailand, Indonesia, and India.

Now an expert in security analysis in Asian markets, Mobius received a life-changing phone call. Investing legend Sir John Templeton, a pioneer in global investing and the founder of the Templeton Funds (later Franklin Templeton Investments), had decided to explore Asia and other emerging markets, and who better to help him than Mark Mobius?

Mobius officially joined Templeton as president of the newly launched Templeton Emerging Markets Fund in 1987.

Trouble is Opportunity

Sir John Templeton once said, "If you buy the same securities as other people, you'll get the same results as other people." Taking these words to heart, Mobius focused his energies on emerging markets in which typical investors hardly ever invest.

Mobius explained, "John became my mentor in many ways. His investment philosophy blends in well with my understanding of human psychology and personality because we both liked to go to unusual places to unlock hidden value. For example, if my goal had been to achieve the same results as everybody else, then I wouldn't have taken the initiative to move to Asia in the 1960s and do something different."

Another of Templeton's well-known pronouncements is "bull markets are born on pessimism, grow on skepticism, mature on optimism and die on euphoria. The time of maximum pessimism is the best time to buy, and the time of maximum optimism is the best time to sell."

"John taught me to think for the long term, focus on the fundamentals, and think independently because the investment world has a herd mentality," Mobius elaborated. "To achieve better results, I was encouraged to go against the crowd, but at the same time always analyze the situation before making a decision. John's approach matched my understanding of social psychology and my previous business experiences."

Templeton, who passed away in 2008, also kept a plaque on his desk that read "trouble is opportunity!"

From his office in Hong Kong, Mobius traveled the world looking for investment ideas for Templeton. He later opened an office in Singapore and in 15 other countries, but he never stays in one location for long.

Traveling more than 250 days a year, home for Mobius usually means a hotel room: "I used to have an apartment in Hong Kong, but I sold it. I now own apartments in Singapore, South Africa, and Malaysia, but since I never really stay in those places for long, I rent them out and stay in hotels instead. I now call Dubai my home, but even then my stays there are short."

In 1987, the Templeton Emerging Markets Fund started out with $100 million. Mobius began to load up on stock positions in Hong Kong, Singapore, Malaysia, Mexico, and the Philippines—the only five emerging markets that were open for investment in those early days. Then Black Monday arrived, and Mobius learned an important lesson in fund management: diversification.

He explained, "The Dow Jones Industrial Average dropped over 20 percent on October 19, 1987—Black Monday. The shockwaves reached Asia, and the head of the Hong Kong Stock Exchange decided to close the local market for four days. When it reopened, our investment positions were down by a third. Because we were so heavily weighted in Hong Kong, this was a real wake-up call. I certainly learned the truth of the old adage 'never put all your eggs in one basket.'"

In the years since, Mobius and his team have limited their investment exposure in any particular region or country. Further, within each region or country, they limit their exposure in any particular sector or company: "We usually apply the so-called '5–40 rule,' which means that the sum of our positions with over 5 percent allocation must be less than 40 percent of the overall portfolio. Also, we have an informal indicator, which is limiting any country-specific exposure to less than 20 to 30 percent. Once it gets above that, we watch our positions very closely."

In line with this increased focus on regional diversification, over the past 25 years, Mobius has also broadened the breadth and depth of his investment radar. As of 2011, his investment team was spread across 17 locations, including Argentina, Brazil, Austria, China, Hong Kong, India,

Malaysia, Poland, Romania, Russia, Singapore, South Africa, South Korea, Thailand, Turkey, the United Arab Emirates, and Vietnam.

His team of 51 investment experts, who represent 26 nationalities and speak 24 languages, has collectively built a research database of more than 23,000 securities in emerging markets all over the world.

Mobius explained, "As we travel, we get new ideas about what's happening in different parts of the world. Sometimes those ideas lead us to our next investment or travel destination, but most of the time we have a very systematic way of generating ideas as we analyze the economic and financial data of different countries and companies from our database. It is important to realize that stock markets fluctuate and undergo booms and busts, but over the long term they reflect the economic growth and stability of their respective countries."

The price-to-earnings (P/E) ratio is a quick and easy way of making comparisons across emerging markets. Although Mobius and his team use it to screen for ideas, they are well aware that the ratio is useful only on a relative basis. For example, if a country has a GDP growth rate of 10 percent and a P/E ratio of 10 times, it is certainly more attractive than a country with the same P/E ratio, but only a 5 percent growth rate.

While considering companies, Mobius and his team also look at a plethora of other indicators, such as price-to-book ratio, return on equity, return on invested capital, profit margins, and earnings per share growth.

"Although sometimes our commentaries on economic growth, inflation, and other economic indicators make it sound like we are very macro driven, I must clarify that macro analysis is just one part of our research. Ultimately, we are bottom-up value investors because we stress the importance of understanding the individual companies in our portfolio. After all, it is individual companies that are the components of our portfolio, not specific countries or regions," he further commented.

Mobius also cautioned that a focus on the macro landscape holds the danger of becoming biased toward a specific region: "We don't want to ignore good companies in bad economies. Sometimes we like troubled economies that are in financial or political distress because they spell opportunity!

"In essence, we look for the next big crash in emerging markets because in value investing, money is made after the crash, not before, so we don't mind seeing crises or downturns. First, we are mentally prepared for them, and, second, we don't mind them affecting our short-term performance because we are here for the long term."

Over the years, Mobius has come to delegate much of the fundamental analysis to his investment research team. A more important role for him is to focus on the qualitative aspects of businesses, which means numerous company visits and meetings with management.

"I respect investors for crunching numbers and then buying and selling stocks based on their financial models. This method, however, only works when there is a sophisticated and transparent accounting system. Nevertheless, deep knowledge of the management is needed," Mobius explained.

"When it comes to emerging markets, you cannot rely on the numbers because they cannot be entirely trusted. You have to go out there and start kicking tires. Then you have to talk to company management, look into their eyes, and determine whether they are reliable. They may say their employees are happy, but sometimes you have to visit the company and talk to competitors to see whether that's really the case. Otherwise the numbers that you input into your financial model are no better than what computer geeks call 'garbage in and garbage out.'"

Of course, Mobius brings more than his evaluation of company quality to his investment team. The team also benefits from his long experience. Based on his business acumen and insight, his job is to balance and maintain a broad perspective on different markets from a historical, current, and future view.

As regional investment specialists tend to favor their own regions, Mobius requires them to take a step back and compare their investment findings locally and regionally. His duty, then, is to ensure capital goes to the right market at the right price and the right time.

"I tell my people always to focus on the long term in their analysis because there are always hot stocks in emerging markets that are either unsustainable in the long run or that turn out to be scams. Our aim is to compare companies, regions, and countries objectively without fear or favor," Mobius said.

Because their minimum holding period for an investment is five years, Mobius and his team have the stomach to tolerate wild market swings: "All markets are fundamentally cyclical. Because emerging markets are somewhat immature, people get overly bullish and bearish all of the time. By focusing on value, we get in when everyone else is trying to get out. Also, our value discipline lets us compare different markets to see which ones are overpriced, so by the time everyone is trying to get in, we are getting out."

Mobius added, "When we look at an investment, we evaluate the company's records for the past five years, and then we project its business for the next five. Because emerging markets technically start from ground zero, things can change quickly, so even if you try to project a business beyond five years, your analysis is likely to become a little vague. However, our holding period of five years leaves us room for market volatility in between. Obviously, there are times when our investments drop after our first purchase, but if we feel confident about the business and its management, then we don't mind buying more as it's on its way down.

"Over the years, we've had a lot of experience with bad weather and rough rides during our travels and company visits, but most of the latter have stemmed from the discovery that company management is cheating shareholders. Such experiences are difficult, but as a result we have become better judges of people, and better investors."

Even in-depth research is not always enough to combat the vagaries of human nature, Mobius said. "When we are cheated, there is not much we can do except to learn from our mistakes and move on. People say emerging markets are dangerous places to invest, but Bernie Madoff operated in the U.S. for years. My belief is that there are good and bad people in every country. All you need to do is to keep an open mind, do your homework, and believe that the world is getting better each day despite the crises that occur from time to time."

Feeling the Market

Mobius has developed four cardinal rules for investing in emerging markets—fair, efficient, liquid, and transparent—which form the acronym FELT.

By "fair," Mobius means that one must make sure that the prospective emerging market treats its investors, both big and small, equally. "Efficient" means determining whether the stock exchange and local brokers are honest and friendly to investors and charge them at competitive and acceptable rates. Finally, an attractive emerging market will have the liquidity to place buy and sell orders on stocks, and these stocks will be characterized by accounting and financial transparency.

Mobius explained: "I have seen stock exchanges that are unfriendly to investors. I have walked into stock exchanges that have only a few people, and the same people operate the stock brokerage next door. I have dealt with dishonest brokers, and been in situations in which we couldn't exit our holdings because of illiquidity in the downward market. And I have seen accounting reports with fake numbers. So, again and again, I stress the importance of visiting companies and sizing up the situation firsthand."

In a nutshell, Mobius believes that there is no simple formula for successful investing. There are no blueprints, no guarantees, and certainly no Holy Grail. There is, however, the right attitude that leads to better investing.

He said, "One important thing I learned from John [Templeton] was humility. By being humble, you are more open to new ideas and can be more objective in your investment research. With an open mind, you can accept that the world changes and that you must constantly learn new things to keep pace with it.

"What keeps me going today is my passion for investment research. It allows me to research the world, which leads me to understanding the meaning of life. To be a good investor, you need to open up your mind and be ready to accept whatever the world has to offer."

Given the nonstop travel their work requires, the Franklin Templeton Group decided it would be safer (particularly given some of the unusual places Mobius needs to visit), cheaper, and more efficient for him and his team to travel by company jet than to take commercial flights. Since the 1990s, Mobius has traveled in style, though he also flies commercial if it is more convenient.

He commented that "the company jet has made us more efficient because we can cover more places faster and also discuss investment ideas together on the way to company visits. It also gives us greater security. As for jet lag, I don't suffer from it anymore because my body clock has no idea what time zone is home!"

Mobius's wide experience of the world allows him to collect local intelligence quickly and smoothly in new locales because he is open to talking to anyone at any time. Having seen the best and worst of emerging markets, he does have some concerns.

"What I dislike most is when I go to a new place and see a lack of laws and regulations that could improve the market and people's lives dramatically. In some cases, there is a need for greater regulation, and in others, less. Greater regulation is needed to improve transparency, but less to promote it," Mobius said.

He explained: "As the investment world is converging in the sense that people are becoming more global in their investment patterns, transparency is becoming increasingly important because investors depend on accurate corporate reporting to evaluate companies. However, I don't see the bureaucracy and politics of different countries changing dramatically in a way that will improve transparency any time soon. I do hope that through my involvement in these markets, I can encourage them to improve their market structure one step at a time. In the meantime, we will not change our investment research approach, although we may change the way it's carried out."

Always at the frontier of new emerging markets, Mobius is a unique value investor who brings something beyond analysis of the numbers. As head of the Templeton Emerging Markets Group, he sees his role as monitoring the winds of change in these markets, as he eloquently explains in his book *Passport to Profits*:

> Things change. The [important thing is] to remain—as a manager, as a messenger, as an investor—fluid and flexible. Markets, like [the] ocean and tides, are a wave phenomenon. The only way to stay on top is to bend your knees, keep your balance, and surf. Like surfing, riding the waves of the global market can be a blast. Not to mention incredibly profitable. But what we look for consistently, as part of our fundamental analysis, is a company's, a country's, a region's, and a management's capacity to *manage change*.

CHAPTER 9

The Value-Oriented Businessman

Teng Ngiek Lian
Target Asset Management

Experience is not what happens to a man; it is what a man does with what happens to him.

—*Aldous Huxley*

Teng Ngiek Lian is the founder of Target Asset Management Pte. Ltd., a long-only investment management company established in Singapore in 1996. The company's flagship Target Value Fund, which invests mainly in Asia ex-Japan, grew from $5.5 million at inception to $2 billion in July 2010, when Teng announced his retirement.

From September 1996 to November 2010, the fund returned 892.44 percent, or 17.59 percent per annum. During the same period, its benchmark index, MSCI ACFE (All Country Far East ex-Japan), returned 81.27 percent, or 4.29 percent annually.

After celebrating his sixtieth birthday, Teng wrote in his retirement letter in July 2010 that he wanted to take a short break to attend to personal matters and to think of ways to practice fund management in a less stressful manner. After a year of relaxation and brainstorming, he came out of retirement in June 2011 and re-launched the Target Value Fund with a smaller initial fund size of approximately $500 million. His objective is to again pursue higher returns and lower risk by applying his time-tested value investing principles.

"Before one can properly determine the valuation of a stock, it is necessary first to determine its business quality," Teng Ngiek Lian explained in a discussion of his investment philosophy. "An absolute low stock price has no meaning if one does not consider its business quality and compare it against its peers. Buying a stock at a low price and subsequently selling it higher without considering its business quality is really just 'value trading,' not 'value investing.'"

A Malaysian-born Chinese who has lived in Singapore since 1985, Teng believes that the art and science of value investing is skewed more toward art than science. "The ability to identify and evaluate a business is the most important part of the battle! Once you are able to understand its business model, identify its critical success factors, and determine its competitive strength (or weakness), financial analysis and valuation become much easier," he said.

A businessman turned fund manager, Teng has the capacity and credentials to talk business and investing at the same time. He believes that being a good value investor comes down to a thorough business understanding and a diversity of life encounters and business dealings. Teng certainly fits the bill.

Learning the Numbers

The son of a wooden clog maker and the sixth of seven children, Teng was born in 1950 in Dungun, a coastal district in the Malaysian state of Terengganu. Growing up in a politically unstable environment in which economic policies were constantly changing, he faced many hardships.

"Because of my poor family background, at a young age I told myself that I had to get out of poverty," Teng recalled. "It was no fun being poor! I was determined that however hard I had to struggle, I had to earn a good living one day. I looked around and saw that most rich people were in business, and so all I wanted to do was to become a businessman and make myself rich."

Forced to leave school at the age of 18 to earn a living, Teng worked part time at a mining company, a timber plantation, and an accounting firm. Learning business concepts at these jobs and taking night classes in accounting, after four years, he had saved enough money to attend college part time in the Malaysian capital, Kuala Lumpur. He worked as an accounting clerk during the day and attended college at night until he was able to qualify as a chartered certified accountant and a chartered secretary.

In 1973, Teng joined the Guthrie Group, one of the leading British-owned conglomerates in Southeast Asia, as a branch accountant. The group was engaged in oil palm and rubber plantations, property development, manufacturing, chemicals, and consumer goods trading, affording Teng the opportunity to get a taste of all of these businesses during his decade in its employ.

Elaborating on his decision to join Guthrie, Teng noted that his plan had always been to start his own business, but because he had married young and had two small children, he had to earn enough money to raise his young family and service his mortgage debt. The rational decision was to work for a large corporation, especially as Malaysia was still an emerging market in which the employment situation could be unstable at times.

Climbing the corporate ladder over the next few years, Teng become chief accountant of one of the group's subsidiaries before being promoted to financial controller and then to chief financial officer of the overall group.

"Because of my senior financial position, I was required to have a good understanding of the group's diverse businesses so that I could analyze their performance. The areas I had to analyze included marketing, distribution, logistics operations, inventory management, and accounts receivable management. By using different financial models to evaluate and project businesses, I made recommendations to the company's board on capital and resource allocation," Teng explained.

"In the process, I was never afraid to ask questions. I would find out who was the most capable person running each division, and then I would befriend him or her and learn how he or she handled the business. Occasionally I would also share my ideas with these individuals based on my evaluation of the business."

From a company's perspective, the accounting division is a cost center. As an accountant, Teng felt that he was more like a housekeeper, and hence his career prospects would be limited. After becoming financial controller, he realized that he could in fact make money for the firm. By managing the group's foreign exchange and sourcing the best financing terms, he slowly became a profit center. For these contributions, he was paid good bonuses and even rewarded with a company car. Gradually Teng became interested in the financial market.

In the early 1980s, the financial community in Southeast Asia was relatively small. Not too happy with the region's business environment, Teng decided to go to Australia to look for opportunities. In 1985, he decided that Southeast Asia was his home after all, so he returned. Rather than return to Malaysia, however, he moved to Singapore, where he joined the publicly listed WBL Corporation as financial controller.

"Moving to Singapore with my family was exciting because the country was becoming a financial hub in Southeast Asia, and its economic and political prospects were the most promising in the region," Teng said. "In this much more sophisticated financial market, I had the opportunity to deal with top investment bankers and network with a more international community."

Founded in 1906, WBL is a Singapore-based multinational conglomerate that operates throughout Asia. As it had a considerable amount of cash and several old economy businesses in the 1980s, the group decided to diversify into new growth industries, such as computer and component manufacturing and agricultural technology.

Joining the conglomerate allowed Teng to learn about its main businesses, which included automobile, heavy machinery, and equipment distribution. In addition, he was given the task of managing the abundance of cash that the company had accumulated over the years. Applying his financial skills, Teng traded foreign exchange, fixed income, and equity for the company.

By the end of the 1980s, WBL had deployed most of its surplus cash into its new business ventures. Now having fewer investment responsibilities, Teng decided to move on. In 1990, he resigned from WBL to become managing director of Morgan Grenfell Investment Management Asia, a leading London-headquartered investment bank.

The Art of Contrary Thinking

Teng's relationship with Morgan Grenfell dated back to the mid-1980s when he represented WBL in placing investment trades. He recalled, "After I had dealt with the investment team at Morgan Grenfell for a while, one of its executives told me that if I ever thought about leaving WBL, I should consider joining them. I think they were probably impressed by my contrarian approach to investing, especially after they saw how I made investments during the Pan-Electric crisis in Singapore in late 1985 when I bought many beaten down stocks while others were panicking."

Pan-Electric Industries was a Singapore-based company specializing in marine salvage work. When the group collapsed in 1985 due to unsettled forward contracts and related party transactions, it had 71 subsidiaries and a connection to virtually every facet of the Singaporean economy. It was wiped out overnight, forcing the Singapore Stock Exchange to close for three days. The crisis was unprecedented in Singapore, and remains so to this day.

"The event was my first taste of a crisis," Teng explained. "At the time, stocks were quite inflated, and Pan-Electric was really the trigger point that caused them all to tumble. Somehow I was convinced to enter the stock market because I had done my research on many companies for a long time, and they finally represented a good buying opportunity.

"I believe my strong conviction was due to my experience in handling different kinds of businesses over the years, which had gained me the insight to tell which businesses were good and bad and whether they were selling at a discount. Moreover, my accounting background also gave me the know-how and discipline to analyze business sensitivities. When even my worst-case scenario assumptions convinced me to buy, I had to trust my research."

Teng was further encouraged by something Benjamin Graham wrote in *The Intelligent Investor*: "You are neither right nor wrong because the crowd disagrees with you. You are right because your data and reasoning are right."

Indeed, Teng was proven correct. Although Singapore's stock market dropped 20 percent after the panic in November 1985, in four to five months' time, it had recovered all of its losses and even begun an uptrend to gain more than 30 percent a year later.

Teng believes that his accounting background has taught him to be conservative when conducting investment research. Therefore, when downside risk is carefully analyzed, the upside naturally takes care of itself. This mindset warns him against excessive optimism in any business because market cycles come and go.

Another contrarian decision witnessed by Morgan Grenfell's investment team was Teng's decision to sell all of his Japanese stocks in early 1989 when the Nikkei 225 index reached 31,000 points. His rationale was that Japanese businesses were priced at extremely optimistic levels. Not being at all greedy, he was satisfied with his investment returns and happy to let go. The index reached its peak at 38,900 points in late 1989 and then tanked the following year, falling by more than 50 percent.

On leaving the corporate world and entering the investment world, Teng commented: "Despite how much Morgan Grenfell's people liked me, I still had to convince them that I was the right person to take the job. I told them that although they could search for other good investment professionals, it would be difficult to find a person like me who also had experience in business development capabilities. I said that with my business experience and knowledge of investing, I was confident that I could develop new investment products more quickly than other qualified investment professionals. Thankfully, they were convinced by my arguments."

Indeed, shortly after joining Morgan Grenfell, Teng brought fresh business insights to his team. "Our team wanted to build some investment funds with popular Asian themes, but we had no track record. Instead of going mainstream and directly competing with the big fund houses, we had to be different. I proposed the idea of launching emerging market funds in which other fund houses had no track record. That way, when we became recognized, we could reintroduce some mainstream products to the market."

Teng's boss took his business proposal seriously. In the next three years, he and his team started funds in Korea, Pakistan, Indonesia, and China. Well received by investors, some of these funds grew from $80 million to more than $600 million in just a few years.

Looking back, Teng acknowledged that investment know-how is only one aspect of the fund management business, and superior investment performance does not necessarily translate into successful fund management. To run a sustainable investment operation, another critical success factor is the capability of business development and management, which can range from raising capital to managing people, marketing the fund, and retaining investors.

In 1993, Teng's immediate boss, Hsieh Fu Hua, the head of Morgan Grenfell Asia, fell out with the London head office, prompting many senior management staff, including Teng, to resign.

He recalled, "I was quickly headhunted by UBS Asset Management (East Asia) while my boss, Mr. Hsieh, and several other colleagues went on to start Prime Partners Group, an investment banking company. In 1994, I left UBS and joined my ex-boss at Prime Partners."

The following year, Teng was presented with a once-in-a-lifetime opportunity: "The Monetary Authority of Singapore changed the regulations on investment advisory bodies, lowering the requirements for starting an investment fund. I said to my boss and my wife right away that I must start my own business because being my own boss had been my childhood dream. Already 45, my age, my investment knowledge, and my business experience all gave me a competitive edge. I knew that if I could build a nice performance record over the next three years, something good would happen."

In 1996, Teng established Target Asset Management with total assets under management of $5.5 million.

Targeting Good Businesses in Asia

Searching for value with the eyes of a businessman, Teng's main objective has always been to find good companies at reasonable prices. Given Asia's dynamic political environment and cultural diversity, Teng cautioned that investors must carefully assess the risks and opportunities in different Asian markets before making any investment decision.

He explained, "Understanding politics is important because a change in political power can lead to a drastic change in economic direction. Because the political systems in many Asian countries are still young, risks and opportunities come and go very quickly.

"The economic cycle is also much shorter in this region, and market volatility is much greater than that in mature economies. In addition to understanding the characteristics of the Asian market, it is also important to understand the mindset of businesspeople in this part of the world."

Reviewing the Asian business environment, it comes as no surprise to find that smart Asian businesspeople are very alert to which way the political wind is likely to blow and to the next business opportunity.

The smart investor needs to differentiate between those getting into a new business for business reasons and those doing so for political reasons. Sometimes it is the businessperson's network and entrepreneurial skills that drive the business rather than the nature of the business itself.

In addition to politics, culture is a concern. Teng noted the diverse cultural characteristics of the region's Chinese-speaking people alone. For example, due to the different political environments in which they live, Hong Kong and Taiwanese citizens generally tend to have a lower risk tolerance than their mainland Chinese counterparts.

When it comes to tastes and preferences, even within mainland China, there can be tremendous diversity. For example, different parts of China have their own dining cultures. When evaluating a food and beverage business, then, what works in northern China may not work in the south.

Teng said, "I spend most of my time trying to understand businesses, identify their success factors, and examine their operational capabilities. Particularly with small- and medium-sized businesses, I like to dig into their operational details such as their distribution logistics, branding and marketing strategy, and financial and cash flow management.

"For example, sometimes I ask management how they deal with their company's stock obsolescence, and if they cannot or refuse to answer the question, or if they spout back a bunch of nonsense, then I would rather stay away from them irrespective of how attractive the business is."

When investing in Asia, many investors focus on the region's growth potential. Beyond focusing on the numbers and statistics, such as a business having 5,000 distribution channels and the capacity to expand into 2,000 more, they must also understand how the business works. For example, what makes the business tick? Why do consumers want its products? What is the right price structure for those products? What is the contingency plan if the products do not sell? These questions must be asked even before the business is valued.

Thanks to his business acumen, Teng focuses on asking the right questions because he knows that in the Asian industry landscape, a well-defined business model and management quality are key. In fact, an investment valuation can be accurate only if these important business issues are identified and addressed.

Teng explained, "Because Asia is a fast-growing region, and there is an abundance of business opportunities, many entrepreneurs become overly ambitious and distracted from their core competence. Also, there is a large corporate governance risk, as legal regulations are not properly enforced in the region. It is therefore very important to have a good network to check the background of these businesspeople, particularly those who have a very short business history."

He added: "In fund management, you cannot look at only one dimension of a company. You also cannot look at a single company and say that it is a good company. If you look at only one company at a time, then you are as good as blind! You must make relative comparisons. After all, how do you know a business is good if you do not compare it with others?

"You must consider the market dynamics and the different characteristics of a business. Here in Asia, even if you find the right industry, you might still lose money. You often have to look into an industry's food chain to see who calls the shots and who owns the sweet spot."

Teng gave an example of how a top retailer in Hong Kong was doing good business, but it still had to close down because the landlord kept raising the rent. "Customers were lining up in front of the shop, and it still had to close down. What does that mean for the investor?" he wondered.

The Relativity of Valuation

As the saying goes, "A good business may not necessarily be a good investment, and a good investment may not necessarily be a good business." Picking a good business is Teng's priority, but when a good one is spotted, investment valuation comes next.

Teng said, "We are given two eyes, one for the upside and the other for the downside! When it comes to valuation, we must first distinguish which growth phase a company is in, and then play with its upside and downside sensitivities. If it is in a high-growth stage, then value comes from the company's prospects, but if it is a no-growth company, then value may come from its share price discount.

"Value is relative. When I do my quantitative analysis, I do not have strict criteria regarding the numbers, such as the P/E ratio has to be less than 10 times, return on equity has to be over 15 percent, or the debt-to-equity ratio has to be such and such. I think a sensible investor has to take into account the characteristics of a business, the economic conditions, the investment environment, and valuations among different potential investments. Flexibility is the key, and it requires experience."

Teng has no objection to buying businesses at the forefront of the new economy as long as they show proof of generating real cash flow. It just takes a bit of foresight and imagination. Without real cash flow, good businesses are nothing but good concepts.

Teng believes that the goal of value investing is to find undervalued opportunities. The problem, however, lies in defining "undervalued." Does an investment have to be undervalued when the investor buys it? Or can it be undervalued in a year's time if the investor has the vision to buy it today?

"I quite often say to investors that despite being a value investor, I do invest in high P/E stocks if the high P/E is due to a passing business phase or a short-term mishap that is unlikely to recur," Teng elaborated. "We like to buy into fallen angels or companies going through necessary growing pains before their earning potential is developed. It is like buying an ugly caterpillar that eventually becomes a butterfly. Being able to make such an investment requires a lot of in-depth research and a good understanding of the business and its industry dynamic."

Teng believes in the value investment strategy developed in the West, but recognizes that it requires adjustments for application in the East because of the highly volatile nature of the region's markets. He explained: "While emerging countries have higher growth, they also have greater risk in terms of politics, corporate governance, the shorter business cycle, and less liquidity. A market correction in an emerging economy can easily mean 20 to 30 percent, which is equivalent to a crash in a developed market.

"Because valuations on stocks can swing wildly, a long term buy-and-hold strategy without due regard to market volatility can lead to underperformance. This is not to say that one should actively trade the market, but it is wise for investors to make a profit when the market is euphoric or a stock has reached its full valuation, and then to buy again when the market corrects."

Teng tends to invest in fewer companies, concentrating on surer bets and devoting more time and his expertise to businesses that he knows well. At any given time, his portfolio consists of roughly 30 stocks. Contrary to the popular adage about "never putting all of one's eggs in one basket," he believes that it is easier and better "to put most eggs in one basket, and then watch that basket!"

A concentrated portfolio allows a fund manager to remain focused, which makes his or her work easier. Teng joked that making the decision to own a stock is to him as serious as saying "I do" in a marriage ceremony. He thus makes a solid case to himself each time he drops or adds a stock to his investment portfolio.

He explained: "If a stock in the portfolio drops, what concerns me most is whether it has fallen along with the broader market or whether it has fallen against its sector. It is natural to fall with the broader market, but if it falls against its peers, then this means the market has concerns about this individual company. I would drill right into the reasons and find out why.

"Sometimes, a stock gets sick for different reasons. If it has only caught a cold, then it may be an opportunity to buy more and average out, but if it has terminal cancer, then I have no hesitation in cutting the stock out right away. Because my strength lies in evaluating businesses, I am not affected by the noise in the market. What I care about most is whether the drop is due to normal business issues or business structural changes."

A Value Lifestyle

Growing up in a low-income family, Teng learned to be frugal at a young age. Over the years, he has learned to make sure that whatever he buys constitutes value for money. He stresses the importance of making comparisons before any purchase, whether for an investment product or anything else. Indeed, looking for value has become a way of life.

In 2006, when office rents in Singapore began to rise, Teng looked into buying his own office. Instead of aiming for a prestigious location, he compared prices and found a bargain just a few minutes away from the fancy commercial buildings in the central business district. He turned an attractive three-story conservation shophouse next to restaurants and fashion boutiques into his fund house. The property's value has gone up tremendously since his purchase.

Teng said, "Shopping and investing are similar. They are really about common sense, but somehow common sense seems to have become quite uncommon. Sometimes, good deals and good ideas come from talking to different people, and then the next step is to think more deeply about those ideas and how they interconnect with our society and economy. When we think hard enough, we sometimes get a sense of what is happening around the world."

He cited the Asian financial crisis of 1997 as an example: "When everyone in the world was praising Asia, I made a conscious effort to sell down Asian stocks because they were quite inflated in the first place. Moreover, many business deals in the region were a matter of ego and ambition."

Three deals in particular set off alarm bells. "The first one was when Malaysia decided to build the world's tallest building, the Petronas Twin Towers," Teng recalled. "The second was when Malaysia and Indonesia had talks about building a bridge to connect the two countries, which would have cost billions of U.S. dollars. The third was when many booming Asian cities were flooded with millions of illegal immigrants all taking part in the frenzy. I could not tell when a crisis would hit, but I knew something was not right."

Managing to duck the crisis, Teng's investment fund dropped only 15.74 percent in 1997 when its benchmark index dropped 44.31 percent. Then, in 1998 when the index dropped 4.82 percent, Teng generated 61.8 percent.

Although common sense saved Teng from danger, it did not ease the pressure placed on him during the Internet boom and bust: "When my clients said how old-fashioned I was for not taking part in the new dot-com economy, I had a second of doubt about whether my investment knowledge had become obsolete or the world had really gone through a structural change. Then I thought more about it and realized that Internet companies were no different from non-Internet companies. They still had to pay tax, interest, salary, rent, and other expenses. Yet they made no real cash."

Indeed, Teng's sensible attitude and good judgment allowed him to generate a 1.44 percent return in 2000 when his fund's benchmark index dropped 36.73 percent.

Moving forward to 2008, the global financial crisis presented Teng with his first real challenge. Following the collapse of Lehman Brothers, even common sense could not protect a long-only value fund.

"The fund outperformed its benchmark, but it was still down by 44 percent," Teng said. "As a value investor, I knew stocks were cheap, but I could not tell when the world would turn around. I wrote a special letter to my investors, telling them that I would personally inject US$10 million into the fund to support my buying thesis. When the worst was over in 2009, the fund was up 68 percent."

Hitting the sixty-year mark in 2010, Teng decided it was time to slow down. He closed down his fund in November of that year, but decided to reopen it just under a year later. "I am just too addicted to investing. It is a way for me to learn and understand life, and it is a way for me to appreciate our vibrant world. Relaunching the fund, I wanted to keep the fund size at about US$500 million and to limit it to fewer clients. I still enjoy running money, but I want to do so in a less hectic manner," he explained.

A value manager who has never subscribed to Bloomberg or Reuters, Teng does not believe in keeping up with minute-by-minute changes in stock prices. After all, value investing is about buying good businesses, and stock price fluctuations have nothing to do with it.

In support of the value lifestyle he leads, Teng concluded, "Our globalized economy has made the world move faster and closer together. Because capital flows around so quickly, diversification is not necessarily going to reduce risk! What matters then is how the investor applies the value investing framework to find good businesses that are sustainable enough to survive any crisis."

CHAPTER 10

Value Investing in the Lost Decade

Shuhei Abe
SPARX Group

In the struggle for survival, the fittest win out at the expense of their rivals because they succeed in adapting themselves best to their environment.

—*Charles Darwin*

*S*PARX *Group Co., Ltd. is a publicly owned asset management holding company in Japan. Its origins date back to 1989, when Shuhei Abe founded SPARX Asset Management Co., Ltd. in Tokyo.*

Focusing on Japanese equity research and investments since its inception, the company has transformed itself over the years from managing a small-cap value fund to long-short and macro-oriented strategies in Japan and throughout Asia. Listed on the JASDAQ Securities Exchange in 2001 under the name SPARX Group, it expanded its footprint to Korea in 2005 and Hong Kong in 2006.

In 2011, SPARX's total assets under management amounted to $6.5 billion. With 170 employees, the company has a team of 49 investment experts located around Asia who search for value opportunities in the region. Its flagship fund, Japanese Equity Long-Short Strategy, which stresses value investing, has returned 145.80 percent since its inception in June 1997. This return equates to an annualized gain of 6.36 percent. During the same period, the Japanese equity market, as represented by the TOPIX index, had a cumulative loss of −24.63 percent, or −1.92 percent annually.

"Throughout my investment management career, my goal has been to provide investment intelligence and solutions to those who want to invest in Japan," said Shuhei Abe, founder of the SPARX Group.

Founded in Japan in 1989, SPARX stands for Strategic Portfolio Analysis Research eXperts. To Abe, the name also signifies the sudden "spark" of an investment idea—the eureka moment.

"To generate that investment spark, an investor needs to remain open and be receptive to new insights and information," Abe said.

In 1985, when he was 31 years old, Abe formed Abe Capital Research in New York. Starting with $30 million in funding from a wealthy Greek coffee business family, the company focused on investing in Japanese equities.

Taking a value investing approach, Abe's first focus was the Japanese railway sector. He found many railway shares to be attractive because investors valued them on the basis of P/E multiples alone, totally ignoring the market value of the assets on the balance sheet.

Railway companies feared that the government would cut fare prices, and so they had purchased a great deal of land over the years to push down profits. When the property market boomed in the 1980s, this land became extremely valuable. Abe's unique insight into the fact that railway shares were trading many times lower than the market value of the land held by the railway companies gave him the conviction to invest heavily in the sector.

However, as Abe Capital Research served only one client, the railway investment focus was underappreciated. To spread the news of his value proposition, Abe decided to send out a research report, titled "Takeover Opportunities in Japan," to ten of the largest U.S. investors he could think of.

One open-minded individual replied—George Soros of the Quantum Fund. "I was surprised when Soros called to inquire about my investment ideas in Japan," Abe said. "I had a two-hour meeting with him afterward, and he gave me $100 million to act as his 'satellite manager.' Considering that the Quantum Fund was about $1 billion in size at the time, he entrusted me with quite a lot of money!"

Abe continued: "Looking back, I think the reason why Soros hired me was because he had the conviction to allocate capital to Japan in the first place. Because he was already in his late 50s, he could not run around and do everything on his own. I was lucky to have sent out the research report at the right time, and he probably found me to be analytical, energetic, and honest, and so he gave me his trust."

Abe's railway investment idea played out well. Despite the Black Monday crash in October 1987, railway stocks were up about five-fold by 1988.

As Soros felt that the Japanese market was reaching its peak in the late 1980s, he decided to pull his capital out of Abe Capital Research in 1988. In the same year, Abe also decided to close down his company in New York, and he returned to Tokyo to launch SPARX Asset Management in 1989.

The two-year working relationship with Soros proved invaluable to Abe: "I would not be doing what I am doing today if not for Soros. Although I did not learn any specific investment valuation models from him, he gave me the opportunity to understand his investment mindset—how he perceives information and evaluates market cycles.

"For example, he taught me how to make contrarian bets by shorting various stocks on Black Monday in 1987, and how to profit if the asset bubble burst in Japan." Abe added: "Although our idea of shorting the market was correct eventually, we were a little too early in the game."

Parting with Soros, however, was a blessing in disguise for Abe, as the incident led indirectly to his return to Japan. He knew that if he were to show his Japanese market intelligence to investors, being in the country would help him to be more competitive. In addition, Abe and his wife, Tomoko, whom he married in 1985, were ready to return home.

A Musical Beginning

Born in 1954 in the northern Japanese city of Sapporo, Shuhei Abe grew up in an entrepreneurial environment. His father, Koji Abe, was an iron factory foreman before he and his wife, Mitsue, decided to start their own ironworks factory in their garage.

Abe recalled, "My memories of my childhood years suggest that my parents were constantly working. I remember my mother always carrying my younger brother on her back while she made and painted bathroom chimneys in the factory. Back then, with coal and charcoal constituting the main sources of household energy, including the heating of bathwater, bathroom chimneys were commonly found in Japanese homes."

In the 1950s, Sapporo was still a small town. The streets were not paved, and horses were still the main source of transportation.

"Everyone was poor, but hardworking. Our spirit was positive. What we were taught at the time was that Japan was a poor country, and the only way to take the country forward was to trade goods with other places," Abe said.

"Because both of my parents worked and had their own small business, we were not that rich, but compared to others, we were relatively wealthy. I remember we were the first family in our neighborhood to have a television set. Whenever there was a sumo wrestling match, everyone would come to our place to watch it on TV."

Abe was the eldest son in the family and had two younger brothers. Although he was conscious of the hardships his parents faced, he always intended to follow in his father's footsteps. However, before making a success of the family business, he wanted to take a life detour and become a musician.

As a child, Abe was a member of his school's choir. With sponsorship from the local television station, the choir performed on a variety of TV programs. Thanks to these public appearances and the encouraging feedback he received, Abe learned to play the guitar and became a country singer as he entered his teens.

"I had been a top student, but my interest in music distracted me," Abe confessed. "I would practice the guitar all day and even sing in the street, and my grades became simply average."

Passion is one thing, but reality is another. Abe knew that he was a good guitarist and a decent singer, but the reality was that it would take a much greater effort to reach the professional level.

He explained, "It is important to have passion, but at the same time you need to judge yourself objectively. I enjoyed music, but I was not up to professional standards.

"I believe that every human being has an artistic gene, and in his or her lifetime can create at least one masterpiece that is globally competitive. However, to become a professional, you need to replicate your talent again and again if you are to have more than one masterpiece. It is the same with investing. You can be passionate about it, but if you want to become a professional investor, you need to develop a system and have the talent to find good investments repeatedly."

Facing the truth, Abe decided to study economics at Sophia University in Tokyo in the hope of learning some business skills before joining his father's company. Although his university courses did not seem particularly challenging, Abe also decided to take a night class to study English. He took an intensive course lasting three hours a day. After two years, only 20 of the 200 or so students in the class managed to pass, and Abe was one of them.

"I think I was able to pass because I had more free time than my classmates. Many of them had to work part-time to support their families, but I was lucky because my father's business was doing well and I did not have to work. Besides, I worked hard in the course because I believed that knowing English would give me more opportunities to do business in other places," Abe said.

Breaking the Language Barrier

With his new language skill set, Abe decided he wanted to explore the world. On the recommendation of his school chancellor, he was able to join an exchange program at Boston State College in Massachusetts.

Then, upon completing his undergraduate education in 1978, he decided to remain in the United States to further his education. He applied for an MBA and was admitted to Babson College in Massachusetts.

"Becoming more serious about business, I studied very hard. After a year of accounting, finance, and economics courses, the three subjects suddenly came together and formed a uniform business structure in my mind. This was an enlightening experience for me because I began to look into company case studies and started trying to visualize their business models by looking into their numbers," Abe recalled.

After nearly three years in the United States and with an MBA in hand, Abe's intention was to return to Japan to assist his father. However, the family company was severely affected by the oil crisis of 1979 and had to undergo bankruptcy-type restructuring.

On his father's advice, Abe decided to gain work experience at a large Japanese corporation. He joined the Nomura Research Institute as a research analyst in the consumer electronics sector in 1981.

"I did not have a clear objective of what I wanted to achieve at Nomura. I only had the humble goal of becoming a better researcher and eventually writing a book. Because I could speak English, I was assigned to the New York office after a year with the company and became an equity broker, selling Japanese equities to American institutions," Abe said.

Learning from the West

Once back in the United States, Abe realized he had no idea how to sell Japanese equities to investment institutions. His only advantages were that he was Japanese and could speak English.

Abe explained, "In the early 1980s, introducing Japanese stocks to American institutions was virtually impossible because they were not interested in the first place. I concluded that brokering individual Japanese stocks was not the right way to attract them. With nothing to lose as a young salesman in my late twenties, I invented the concept of 'portfolio selling,' and luckily Nomura saw the value of it."

"Instead of selling individual Japanese stocks, which may have seemed too foreign and risky to investors, I studied research reports and analyzed all of the stocks that were recommended by our research team. Thinking as a portfolio manager, I then structured a portfolio and showed it to potential clients. Fortunately, my portfolio had gone up each time I showed it to them, and so little by little I gained new accounts."

Abe believes that when an investment rationale is sound, all that is required is patience and persistence. The same holds true of sales and marketing.

After more than a year of portfolio selling, Abe heard that the State of Tennessee was looking into diversifying its investment portfolio outside the country, so he traveled to Nashville to show the investment team his model portfolio. After meeting with the team every month for a full year, he opened a $50 million account for the Tennessee state government.

"I believe the investment managers in Tennessee were impressed by my persistence and honesty. Even though they gave me no business initially, I took the initiative to meet with them every month. In the end, they were convinced by my model portfolio, and their account turned me into Nomura's most productive Japanese equity broker," Abe recalled.

While selling his portfolio in the American market, Abe noticed that Japanese brokers usually had the misconception that American investors wanted only to deal with Japanese blue chips, such as Sony or Toyota. In fact, this was not the case, particularly where value investors were concerned.

"Fred Reams of Reams Asset Management in Columbus, Indiana, who manages pension money, taught me about value investing and how to look into the balance sheet and to value hidden assets," Abe explained.

"He taught me to think beyond the Japanese way of valuing stocks, to disregard all of the blue chip recommendations by Nomura, and to come up with my own list of stocks that fit his value proposition. That was my first introduction to value investing."

Abe then came across Fidelity Investments. Meeting the owner of the company, Ned Johnson, and subsequently getting to know its star fund manager, Peter Lynch, and Lynch's then protégé, George Noble, Abe began to gain insight into how American investors apply fundamental research to stocks.

Applying the American model, Abe soon came to realize how simplistic Japanese investors had been in their investment research. For example, in the 1950s and 1960s, Japanese investors looked mainly at dividend yields based on companies' book value. Because they overlooked earnings growth, many stocks such as Sony traded as low as 2 to 3 times P/E.

When sophisticated foreign investors discovered these bargain Japanese stocks, the country was gradually introduced to the concept of P/E multiples, which then became the mainstream valuation metric in the 1970s and 1980s.

"In my experience, Western investors have a sophisticated way of valuing stocks. Although they do not normally change their way of looking at things, they apply that way of thinking to find opportunities around the world," Abe commented.

"Learning to become a value investor when I was still inexperienced in the 1980s, I had to change my way of thinking to fit the American model. I had to alter my method of cooking so they could eat it. If they did not like sashimi [raw fish], I might have to cook it. That was survival! When I started up SPARX, it also became my mission to use American valuation models to analyze Japanese stocks so that investors worldwide could better understand and appreciate the Japanese market."

Applying his new mind-set, Abe found bargains in Japanese non-life insurance companies. By looking into the balance sheet and digging into their assets, he discovered that many of these companies had huge portfolios of stock holdings that were worth many times more than their market capitalization. These companies were trading at market average P/E multiples, but had a breakup value many times greater than their share prices; many investment institutions agreed with Abe about their attractiveness.

After making a few successful investment recommendations, Abe started up Abe Capital Research in 1985, and then SPARX Asset Management in 1989.

The Evolution of SPARX

When he founded SPARX at the tail end of the 1980s, Abe found that Japanese brokers had become very complacent about the broader market. As stocks had done very well since 1986, investors found no reason to alter their investment mind-sets. They believed that trading in and out of blue chip stocks would make everyone rich, and no improvement was necessary.

Abe said, "I found that no research was done on small Japanese companies because expanding into this category was a marginal business for large institutions. With the hype in Japan, even rational investment managers were forced to invest in the country, driving large-cap stocks to 70 to 90 times P/E.

"I knew that if I wanted to compete, I had to be different. Therefore, my strategy was to apply value investing to small-cap companies. Because these shares were more illiquid and brokers never attempted to pitch them to clients, they were trading at huge discounts with multiples in the low teens."

Abe created a small-cap model portfolio and began to sell it to large foreign institutions with large-cap exposure in Japan.

His rationale was that large-caps were already trading at hefty premiums. Hence, if institutions did not own small-caps, then either portfolios would become vulnerable in a downturn or, if the market kept rising, small-caps would eventually become a value play. The idea was taken seriously by a sovereign wealth fund in the Middle East, and SPARX was fortunate enough to raise $100 million from the group.

Although founding SPARX was a natural step forward for Abe, he entered the market at the tip of the Japanese asset bubble. Six months later, Japan's main stock market index, the Nikkei 225, began to tumble. Fortunately, Abe's small-cap strategy survived the storm.

He remarked: "December 1989 was the peak for the Nikkei. For small-caps, however, the index was only at 1,600 points and peaked a year later at 4,100 points. There was a time gap before investors began to realize that the main market was not working and decided to put their money into an alternative market, mainly small-caps. Luckily, we benefited from that window of opportunity. Whatever we touched went up!"

The darkest period for SPARX, and Abe, came later in 1992. With the small-cap index, the over-the-counter JASDAQ market, declining rapidly in 1993, the company's revenues were barely sufficient to pay its analysts' salaries and Tokyo's high rents.

"Looking back, I should have realized that our chance of survival was close to zero. But I was still young and passionate, and my fighting spirit told me that I should not give up because I believed in my investment principles," Abe recalled.

New funding from Warburg Pincus in 1994 revived the company's hopes, but investing during Japan's "Lost Decade" remained painful. In 1997, SPARX lost 20 percent of its managed capital while its benchmark index lost 41 percent.

Abe explained, "The market was declining. We were up for a couple of years, then down again. We always found ourselves back at ground zero. Theoretically, if the market is down by 20 percent and we are down by only 10 percent, our clients should be happy. But realistically, they are never happy because we are still down!

"In a crisis, value investors should be happy because they can buy cheap stocks, but in reality clients are always worried. To continue to bring Japanese market solutions to investors, we had to evolve. We had to build new trading skills that would allow us to fulfill clients' real needs—to preserve capital and generate positive returns. Accordingly, in 1997, we became one of the first to launch a long-short fund."[1]

Abe elaborated: "Japan in the 1990s was at a very peculiar point in its history. 'Deflation' was a concept we learned in economics. We never thought it would happen, but it did in Japan. In a deflationary system, investors should not, in theory, own equities because margins will contract as revenues decline while costs do not necessarily drop.

"In such a market environment, the only way to survive is to adjust, to change! By applying value investing to identify both bargain stocks and overpriced stocks, we were able to benefit from both a bullish and bearish stock market."

Although such a long-short strategy seems to deviate from traditional value investing, Abe defended his logic: "I think a good investor has to evolve his strategy over time to fit the market. But at the same time, he must be consistent with his investment philosophy and principles.

"If you look at Warren Buffett, his strategy is different from Benjamin Graham's original value investing principles. If he had not evolved, he would not have found great investments such as Coca-Cola. He improved his strategy by monetizing brand value, which was not a traditional value principle at the time."

Building a Westernized Asia

Abe's logic paid off. SPARX became a market force in the late 1990s and 2000s, and is one of the largest investment institutions in Asia today. Although his strategy is value and his primary focus is Japan, Abe does not confine himself to the strategies he has developed.

He said, "As an entrepreneur, a value investor, and a believer in Japan and Asia, I envision my company as bringing a universal value

---

[1] A long-short strategy involves buying positions that are anticipated to outperform the market or increase in value (long) and to short sell positions that are expected to underperform the market or go down in value (short). The goal is to generate positive returns in both up and down markets.

judgment to different types of investors, breaking the barriers of culture, customs, and language.

"At the same time, we should not be complacent. We have to challenge ourselves to be creative and innovative. Otherwise, the market will abandon us through its own natural selection process."

For Abe, innovation is essential: "Businesses assume that capitalism works, but this ideology was developed in the West, not the East. The entrepreneurial spirit believes that capital has a cost, and the goal is to outperform that cost to create value. However, this way of thinking does not exist in traditional Asian cultures because the cost of capital was provided by the government to facilitate business and trade in ancient times. What is finally happening today is that Asian economies are freeing themselves from their old, non-capitalized structures, and so we must innovate to keep up with this change.

"Besides, if you look at Japanese culture, the dominance of the *keiretsu* [conglomerates of different businesses with inter-locking relationships] has traditionally made Japanese investments unattractive because management serves its own interests, not those of shareholders. In order to improve, we need to bring businesses and the corporate culture forward."

To promote and bring unity to the Asian market, Abe developed a Japan Value Creation Investment Strategy Fund in 2003. SPARX also teamed up with the California Public Employees' Retirement System (CalPERS) and San Diego–based Relational Investors to promote corporate governance in Japan.

By stressing earnings quality, business core competency, cost management, and shareholder value, SPARX became a new force in the market, facilitating and improving corporate governance in many Japanese companies. Not only has the fund generated hefty returns over the years, but it has also changed the domestic corporate culture in Japan.

To expand its investment footprint, SPARX purchased an asset management company called Cosmo in Korea in 2005. Then, in 2006, it acquired PMA Investment Advisors Limited in Hong Kong.

Abe believes that SPARX's expansion was a natural step in its evolution toward becoming an Asian investment house. In his words: "Our goal is to raise and strengthen the caliber and competency of our core franchise. Just like Coca-Cola—people buy it because it equates to quality, reliability, and a good reputation. When people seek investment services in Asia, we want them to think of SPARX as a quality brand they can trust."

Searching for Value

Value investing, to Abe, is locating the potential arbitrage opportunity between an investment's true worth and its market price: "You have to ask yourself: Why does this business make money? What is its sweet spot? Then, you take the management perspective and consider how much the business is worth. Investment analysis is both art and science."

He explained further, "The artistic or qualitative side of investing is probably innate, but then experience can sometimes improve upon nature. For example, the way Warren Buffett judges his managers is an art, but he has improved upon that art as he has gained more life experience."

One thing Abe has learned over the years is that one has to stay focused. Instead of understanding and analyzing different types of investments, the wise investor should remain dedicated to a particular asset type, and find the one that best suits his or her personality and risk tolerance. Abe put it this way: "Maybe I would enjoy looking into bonds or other countries, but my focus has always been Japanese stocks. That is my market intelligence.

"In addition to focus, an investor also requires vision. You need to be a visionary in times of opportunity or crisis because you cannot analyze the world in a linear fashion. While you have the facts, which are based on the past, you need to visualize the consequences, which will take place in the future."

The scientific or quantitative aspect of investing is a skill set that can be nurtured. Abe explained that when he first started SPARX, the company could not afford to hire experienced staff. Japanese culture also hindered the firm's ability to hire talent from good schools, because such graduates traditionally are averse to taking the risk of working for small, unknown companies. Accordingly, Abe had to build his team slowly and groom his analysts one at a time.

Abe said he felt like a high school coach, guiding young individuals in taking a systematic approach to analyzing companies. Eventually, they became experienced analysts who supported the early growth of SPARX.

He added, "Investing is also about establishing a well-defined strategy. At the same time, you must never let numerical targets or the desire to chase investment returns for the sake of it to hijack your principles and strategy.

"When an idea comes to you, you need to brainstorm, to be creative, think about the past and future, and test your thesis. Then, you need to have a systemized way to analyze the potential worth of the investment and how much return you can generate from it.

"When investigating a stock, I look at all of the simple measures that any ordinary investor would ask about. Then, I want to find out how much the investment should be worth in two to three years' time. We want to test our assumptions, play with the sensitivities of our assumptions, and set a target for the investment. Unlike the market, which defines 'long term' as a one-month time period, we want to focus on the merits of the underlying business.

"Although we can project earnings many years ahead, these numbers can become vague and meaningless because the world is uncertain and constantly changing. As a value investor, my aim is to project the worth of a business up to three years. Anything after that becomes a speculative exercise."

To generate investment insights and ideas, Abe and his team meet most Thursdays at 7:00 A.M. for a one- to two-hour brainstorming session over coffee and breakfast. He calls it the "Buffett Club."

This brainstorming session allows the company's analysts and portfolio managers to challenge one another freely over stock ideas and economic viewpoints. Sometimes they even discuss their favorite investment books to spark insights. Abe's favorites include Benjamin Graham's *The Intelligent Investor* and George Soros's *The Alchemy of Finance*.

Abe said, "When conflicting viewpoints arise during the session, we return to the original aim of the debate, refocusing on the numbers and figures. Sometimes the artistic side of the brain makes a good case for the future, but sometimes it is the scientific side. The future has no right or wrong, so it is important to set an objective and to balance out all assumptions. Of course, common sense and experience should not be forgotten."

Reflecting on his life, Abe said he appreciates the immense opportunities Japan has provided him with. Although the harsh realities of the business environment over the years made every step he took uncertain, he learned that luck is only a bonus in the investment business and that over-confidence is an ingredient of failure.

The hardship of selling Japanese equities in the early days, the founding of SPARX during the hype of the asset bubble, and the subsequent adjustments in investment strategies effectively nurtured Abe to become an investment manager, and human being, who understands the feelings of others. In this sense, hard work, honesty, and the utmost sincerity are the virtues that Abe relentlessly upholds.

As the world was beginning to recover from the Internet bubble, the 9/11 terrorist attacks, and the severe acute respiratory syndrome (SARS) outbreak, Abe wrote this passage in October 2003: "Tomorrow is a continuous flow from yesterday and today, while the key is to always do your very best, day after day while never cutting corners along the way. Within the repetition of this trial-and-error process, tangible patterns will gradually come to view. In the beginning, the insights will be vague and ill defined. But in time, this will change to a sense of more concrete confidence and conviction!" Indeed, this is the spirit of SPARX and the motto of value investor Shuhei Abe.

CHAPTER 11

Eternal Sunshine of the Value Mind

V-Nee Yeh
Value Partners Group

It is easy in the world to live after the world's opinion; it is easy in solitude to live after our own; but the great man is he who in the midst of the crowd keeps with perfect sweetness the independence of solitude.

—*Ralph Waldo Emerson*

V-Nee Yeh is the co-founder of Value Partners Limited, a Hong Kong—based asset management company established in 1993 that applies value investing principles to identify investment opportunities in the Asia—Pacific region. The company reorganized itself as Value Partners Group Limited in 2006 and listed its business on the Hong Kong Stock Exchange in 2007.

In 2011, the company was ranked the largest asset management company in Asia, managing a total of $7.2 billion. Its most notable fund, the Value Partners Classic Fund (A Units), had returned 1,756.4 percent since inception in April 1993, an annualized return of 16.9 percent. During the same period, its benchmark index, the Hong Kong Hang Seng Index, had returned 262.4 percent, or an annualized gain of 7.1 percent.

Since stepping down from the day-to-day management of Value Partners in 1996, Yeh's mission has been to spot new investing talent across Asia. In 2002, he co-founded and became chairman of Argyle Street Management—an investment company that seeks opportunities in distressed and special situation Asian investments using a value investing approach. In 2003, Yeh joined Cheetah Investment Management Group as chairman to restructure the group into a fund *of funds that identifies value investing managers and incubates value funds with Asian investment themes.*

"My first real encounter of a market panic was Black Monday on October 19, 1987, when the Dow dropped more than 20 percent," V-Nee Yeh recalled. "I was convinced that the world's economy would be falling into a severe recession, but shortly after, I was proven totally wrong with my outlook."

Just 28 years old at the time, Yeh realized that making macroeconomic predictions was simply too difficult for him. In hindsight, one may be able to tell what is right or wrong, but economic events occur and change so rapidly that even solid facts and figures can often lead to inaccurate judgments.

Rather than focusing on economic figures, Yeh decided to devote more of his attention to individual companies because their fundamentals are easier to understand.

"What I learned after Black Monday was that when a crisis hits, business sustainability is the biggest insurance against a downturn. In that sense, the cash flow generation in a business is the most fundamental and rational basis for determining value," Yeh explained.

Believing that independent thinking, a contrarian approach to investing, and the courage to act in extreme market conditions make life more fruitful, Yeh has the personality traits of a true value investor. Before becoming one, however, he never intended to join the investment world.

A Multidisciplinary Path

Born in 1959, Yeh grew up in a prominent and respectable family in Hong Kong, although he is too modest to admit it. He merely mentioned that his parents, Meou-Tsen and Zung-Sing, are refugees from Shanghai. His grandfather, Kan-Nee, owned a well-established construction company there before moving to Hong Kong in 1937 due to the political uncertainty in China. Abandoning almost everything, the Yeh family arrived in Hong Kong and started a new life from scratch.

At a young age, Yeh was inculcated with a sense of value and humility. He explained: "Although I have been quite privileged, my family has always been thrifty. When I was young, I had limited pocket money and had to be responsible enough to budget and live within my means. My younger sister and I were taught about the meaning of money and materialism. After all, given the early hardship in my family's history, we were told not to get carried away in good times and flushed out in bad times."

During his school years, Yeh had a busy schedule, filled with schoolwork, tutoring, and sports. Apart from his interest in reading comic books and Chinese *Wuxia* fiction[1] to stimulate his imagination, he was always competitive at school.

Yeh left Hong Kong at the age of 16 to study in the United States, where he attended Milton Academy in Massachusetts and graduated cum laude in 1977. He then concentrated on Marxist history at Williams College, graduating magna cum laude in 1981 with a bachelor's degree in history.

Explaining how he chose his college and subject of study, Yeh said: "When I was young, I had no dreams. I had no idea of what I wanted to become and what I wanted to achieve. I decided to attend Williams College simply because it is a liberal school, and being liberal was kind of cool in the 1970s."

After graduating, Yeh decided he did not yet want to work. To prolong his time in school, he decided to study law at Columbia University: "I knew that my history major would not find me a job, and I had no intention of studying the same subject at a higher level. Being liberal and all, I did not want to study business. The least of all evils, then, was to go to law school."

Although many decisions may seem silly at the time, looking back, they often intertwine with one another to form a broader framework.

Drawing on his leftist leanings and belief that a classless society should provide opportunities for all without prejudices due to birth, class, race, or background, in his law studies Yeh wanted to explore how different constitutions juristically shape the behavior of different

---

[1] *Wuxia* is a genre related to the adventures of martial artists.

societies. By investigating such a subject, perhaps he could find meaning in life and discover a career path.

In his pursuit of the law, however, Yeh soon became interested in another subject: "During my law studies, I clerked for two summers. Those experiences strongly showed me that my personality was not suited to becoming a lawyer. One semester, however, I took a securities regulation class and had the opportunity to learn from some investment bankers. I found investment banking intriguing and decided I wanted to try out corporate finance."

Despite his newfound interest, Yeh managed to graduate from Columbia Law School in 1984 as a Harlan Fiske Stone Scholar—one of the highest academic honors the school confers. After passing the California Bar Exam at the age of 25, he accepted an offer to join investment bank Lazard Frères in New York.

Yeh now had to face his first challenge in the real world without any formal finance or accounting training to draw on. Admitting that it was "swim or sink" in his first six months on the job, he had to outwork everyone else just to survive. Fortunately, with his multidisciplinary background, competitiveness, and all-around academic excellence, he excelled under pressure and managed to keep up with the ever-changing and fast corporate pace.

At the New York branch of Lazard Frères, Yeh first worked in the corporate finance division, and then switched to specializing in mergers and acquisitions. In 1988, he was relocated to London as a proprietary trader in risk arbitrage.[2] Then, in 1989, he was named partner of Lazard Brothers Capital Markets.

Recalling his days at Lazard, Yeh noted: "Because the firm was less structured than big investment banks, I was allowed to delve into areas of my own interest, moving from one division to another. To this day I am grateful for the variety of opportunities that were given to me, especially when senior partner Peter Smith from the corporate finance division took a chance on recruiting me even though I had no finance background."

---

[2] Risk arbitrage is a trading strategy that involves the simultaneous purchase of shares in one company and the short sale of another company. The strategy is typically used in expectation of the pending announcement of a company takeover or merger.

Although Yeh gained investment knowledge from different senior partners at the firm, he said that his most memorable investment lesson came from his own folly: "The first trade of my career came from the recommendation of a cold-call broker. He pitched pork belly futures of some sort, and I listened. Soon enough, I lost two months' salary. The lesson was painful but crucial in my investment career, as I learned the importance of doing my own due diligence before buying anything and to never take anyone's investment advice at face value!"

Looking back, Yeh realizes that his freedom in choosing his early path was mainly due to his father's unconditional support, for which he is grateful: "By the Chinese standard of my father's generation, my father was very open-minded. He never insisted that I go into the family business, and he told me that as long as I was passionate in what I did, then he would be fully supportive. His hands-off approach put me under no pressure, but indirectly he shaped me into a more responsible person!"

Indeed, when the Yeh family's company, Hsin Chong International, had to go through a series of corporate restructuring, Yeh felt that it was his duty to return home and assist his father. In 1990, he resigned as a partner at Lazard and officially moved back to Hong Kong.

Seeking a Comfortable Price

The Yeh family decided to restructure its business operations after the Tiananmen Square crackdown in 1989. Confidence in China was badly shaken, and many of Hong Kong's businessmen were worried, especially because Hong Kong would be handed over to China in 1997.

Yeh explained: "Our company was a small entity listed on the stock exchange. The company engaged mainly in property construction, development, and management, and it also ran a shipping business. Since my father's siblings were worried about Hong Kong's future, we had to think of the best solution to bring liquidity to all of our shareholders. If we wanted to treat everyone fairly, we had to restructure our businesses."

In a series of transactions, Yeh split his family's holding company into two entities: Hsin Chong Construction Group and Hsin Chong International Holdings. Then, in 1992, he structured a leveraged management buyout deal to take Hsin Chong International Holdings private.

This transaction quickly brought Yeh fame, as the financial community applauded his astute financial skill set and perfect market timing.

"In hindsight, we were very lucky because the buyout price that we offered was favorably received by minority shareholders. Given that the Tiananmen Square incident still overshadowed market sentiment in early 1992, our offer was considered very fair. If we had tried to squeeze our shareholders and delayed the transaction by six months or so, the deal probably would not have gone through because market sentiment changed positively after Deng Xiaoping made some bullish comments on the country during his southern China tour," Yeh said.

In March 1992, China's then paramount leader, Deng Xiaoping, made a historic visit to Guangdong Province, which neighbors Hong Kong. During this visit, he made bold comments about market reforms to reassure investors and instill confidence. His catchphrase, "To get rich is glorious," ignited interest in investing in Chinese-speaking markets, such as Hong Kong, Taiwan, and Singapore. At the time, Morgan Stanley analyst Barton Biggs even said he was "maximum bullish" on the Chinese economy.

Catching the rise in investment valuation in late 1992 and 1993, when Hong Kong's Hang Seng Index rose more than 30 percent, Yeh was able to repay the debt he had raised for the management buyout by selling the company's shipping fleet, leaving the remaining assets of the newly privatized company with a zero cost base. This transaction further boosted Yeh's reputation as a market genius.

He commented, "The deal looked as if we were good at market timing, but it was really just being fortunate and propitious. Looking back, what I learned is that in deal making, or in investing, you can never tell what the best price is. All you can do is to come up with a price that you are comfortable with, and not second guess what other people think or what the market thinks."

Finding a Value Partner

After reorganizing the family business, Yeh looked for new opportunities in Hong Kong. Although he still enjoyed reading comic books and had taken up skiing, neither was a viable career option. After some thought, he realized that his ultimate passion was investing.

"I did not know what value investing was in the early 1990s. All I knew was that I enjoyed doing my due diligence and making sure that I did not overpay for an investment. Exchanging ideas with different people, one day I was introduced to my future business partner, Cheah Cheng-Hye. As we enjoyed each other's viewpoints and investment philosophy, I came to realize that we were, in effect, value investors," said Yeh.

Cheah, a native of Penang, Malaysia, started his career as a journalist. In 1989, he joined the Hong Kong branch of Morgan Grenfell, a London-headquartered investment bank, to conduct investment research on small- and medium-cap companies in Asia.

When Yeh was privatizing Hsin Chong International Holdings, Morgan Grenfell was the financial advisor to the company's minority shareholders. Cheah, as research director, was responsible for listing the deal's pros and cons on behalf of these shareholders.

Yeh has nothing but praise for Cheah: "I did not know Cheng-Hye when we were privatizing Hsin Chong, but I came to respect him after reading his report regarding our offer. I found his due diligence and investment rationale very impressive and insightful. Representing the other party, he discussed his valuation fairly and stated his viewpoints clearly."

He later got to know Cheah better, and the two friends came up with the idea of forming an investment company, which they duly did, co-founding Value Partners in 1993. Yeh recalled, "We started our first fund, Value Partners Classic Fund, with $5.6 million. With Cheah, myself, and one secretary, we sublet a small room in my family's office. That was how it all started."

He further elaborated, "If you ask me what we wanted to achieve, we really had no clue. All we wanted to do was to invest our own money, accept clients' money if they believed in us, and apply value investing to look for under-followed and under-researched small-cap companies in Hong Kong."

Reviewing the investment landscape in the 1990s, Yeh noticed that even though Hong Kong was already an important financial hub in Asia, domestic investors had quite short-term outlooks and were speculative. Not many of them had prudent investment strategies, and their stock ideas came primarily from rumors and tips.

The big institutions from the United Kingdom and the United States, in contrast, were mostly making their investment decisions from afar.

Rather than focusing purely on stock picking, their strategy was to buy blue chips and large-cap stocks to track the broader market. In effect, they were more like global macro investors than real stock pickers. Moreover, their investment holding periods were not very long term.

Yeh said: "Value investing was a relatively virgin landscape in Hong Kong when we launched our first fund. We did not find any competitor doing the same thing. By focusing on fundamental analysis, we tried to understand the corporate structure of companies, their business model, their cash flow management, and then we came up with the fair value of these companies as if we were going to take them private. We focused on the downside, and then we tried to buy them when they traded at discounts."

He further elaborated on his investment logic: "Investing requires a broad and lateral mindset. When looking for an investment opportunity, the first thing that comes to my mind has always been the cash yield. I always like to know how much cash a business generates. Evaluating the downside risk, free cash flow generation is what ultimately bails out a company in an adverse business environment.

"When it comes to selling, I always think about reinvestment risk. I think the biggest lesson I learned as a value investor is that most people under-price and under-analyze reinvestment risk because even if you make a good investment and sell it, eventually you have to reinvest that money. Since this reinvestment skill is vastly underestimated, the real distinction between a good and average investor is really that the former constantly has good ideas about reinvesting capital to create a compounding effect.

"Finally, holding for the long term and looking for under-followed small-caps, we started Value Partners with this motto: 'Investing through discipline.' To us, this saying is not a slogan to raise money or for promotion. We really mean it! We strongly believe that a value investor needs to be disciplined, and this quality has to be proven through time and through constant practice."

Through disciplined investing, Value Partners has not only grown its assets under management to almost $9 billion (as of 2011), it has also transformed itself into a stronger and better market player by weathering crisis after crisis.

As Hong Kong has long been one of the most liquid markets in Asia, with capital flowing in and out freely, this unique financial center has always been affected by crises of some sort, whether domestic or international in origin.

Yeh commented, "In less than two decades of operation, we have gone through around five market cycles. Every two to three years, we have experienced a crisis, and we have emerged from each of them. These crises have given us more confidence, and have proven to us that value investing works."

Looking back, Yeh realizes that he has found his investment journey both fun and challenging. However, two periods gave him great cause for concern. One was a financially challenging period, and the other was psychologically exhausting.

He recalled: "The 1997 Asian financial crisis and its aftermath were tough. We had a lot of fund redemptions, and it was a touch-and-go moment for Value Partners. With the stock market dropping over 50 percent, the Hong Kong government rescued it by buying a substantial portfolio of local blue chip stocks to sustain the currency peg between the Hong Kong dollar and the U.S. dollar. Since our holdings were mainly in mid- and small-caps, we were left in the dark. These stocks traded at as low as 3 times P/E, and the pressure was intense, but luckily we endured it.

"Psychologically, we were frustrated during the dot-com bubble in the late 1990s and in early 2000. Because we were disciplined enough not to get into technology stocks, we were being laughed at and challenged by clients. With less than 1 percent of our portfolio in technology-related stocks, we survived the crash and proved that discipline was key.

"Prior to the Internet bubble bursting, we were holding China B-shares,[3] which nobody wanted. When the Chinese government opened up the B-share market to domestic Chinese investors, our portfolio went up 80 percent while the market tumbled 50 percent."

---

[3] China B-shares are common stocks listed on the Shanghai and Shenzhen stock exchanges. These stocks are denominated in Renminbi but settled in either U.S. or Hong Kong dollars. Before 2001, B-shares were limited to foreign investors, but after February 19 of that year, they became freely tradable by domestic Chinese investors.

Spotting Value Minds

In addition to a busy business life, Yeh has had a busy personal life. He married Mira Leung in 1994, and they had a daughter, Nadya, in 1996. In the year his daughter was born, Yeh made the decision to step down from the management of Value Partners. Leaving co-founder Cheah Cheng-Hye as manager, Yeh became honorary chairman and remains in close touch with the company to share insights and ideas.

Yeh explained his rationale: "Cheng-Hye has been the chief investment officer from day one, and he should be credited for most of Value Partners' success. I was honestly just a partner who bounced ideas off him. Besides, having a trustworthy partner like Cheng-Hye, the best strategy was to leave him in charge and let him do what he does best!"

Yeh admitted that he is well aware of his weakness. "I know I am more of an entrepreneur than a real fund manager. Although I am very passionate about investing, I do not have the killer instinct that a good fund manager has. However, I am always the second man in the team to show support because my vision is for the long term."

Yeh had other reasons for stepping down from the management of Value Partners. In 1996, he was asked to sit on the listing committee board of the Hong Kong Stock Exchange. To avoid any potential conflict of interest, distancing himself from the day-to-day activities of Value Partners was the logical choice. Yeh was also asked to oversee the family business, and decided it would be unfair to all parties concerned if his attention were divided.

While running the family business, Yeh continued to look for investment opportunities. In 2002, he co-founded another Hong Kong–based investment management company—Argyle Street Management—which focuses on investing in distressed assets.

Yeh explained: "I found two partners, Kin Chan and Angela Li, who exhibit very similar personality traits and a similar value investing philosophy to Cheng-Hye, except that they engage in a different asset class and have different investment methodologies. Recognizing how talented and committed they are, I realize I was very lucky to team up with them. I was hands-on when the company was first set up, but once it gained traction, I learned to let go and let them run the business."

Of his decision to step back from the front line to become the manager of investment managers, Yeh commented: "I think many investors and even investment books like to discuss what the right investment style or method is, but I do not think we should get too bogged down with what is the right or wrong way in the first place. Instead, it is more appropriate to understand oneself before deciding on a specific investment style.

"If you are a calm and patient person, then the value investing approach may be right for you; but if you are jumpy and aggressive, then a more trading-oriented style may be more suitable. Investing is not about finding a fixed form, but about understanding your temperamental compatibility towards investing and improving your strategy through time and experience. Otherwise, you are always fighting against yourself!"

Drawing on this belief, Yeh continued to look for new investment talent who shared his philosophy but applied different strategies in the market. In 2003, he joined Cheetah Investment Management as chairman to identify and incubate investment funds with different Asian investment themes. On the basis of value investing principles, he and his partners have launched a number of different funds within the Asia—Pacific region.

"Picking good investment managers is an art. Having partnered up with many value people for the past 17 to 18 years, I have developed something of an intuition about the body language of true value managers who mean what they practice. To me, it has almost become a matter of osmosis to understand their thinking and perspectives," Yeh said.

"Good managers can deliver real long-term value, but we have to look beyond their latest performance records and understand their true personality and style first. Sometimes even when the personality and strategy of a manager make sense, performance may lag due to the stage of an economic cycle, so patience and a longer term investment horizon are required."

Becoming a Man of Value

Living in Hong Kong and seeing the influx of foreign capital due to the anticipated benefits of China's economic growth, Yeh has experienced the meaning of globalization first-hand.

Commenting on the so-called East–West divide, he said, "The world is getting smaller, and we should not make too much of the cultural difference between the East and the West anymore because globalization and the Internet have led to a convergence in the mindset of the younger generation.

"In terms of investing, the West has already developed its own method of valuation, while the East is still in the early stages of developing its own investment culture and mentality. Obviously value investing is a good way to go, but it takes time for the average investor to understand its principles. As Asians also tend to have a disproportionate amount of their savings in property, the equity market still has a lot of room to expand, particularly when the upcoming middle class, mainly in China, begins to allocate capital to stocks."

Looking ahead, what concerns Yeh is global uncertainty, with the growing possibility of tail events, which—aggravated by the wrong political decisions—could easily send the world's economy into a tailspin. Since the fall of Lehman Brothers in 2008, for example, economic sentiments have been affected more by political issues than by financial ones.

Yeh commented: "In many situations, economists have proposed good ideas for how things can be done, but political constraints, as well as different political motives, have always ruined these good ideas. Although the world has become more uncertain and global markets have become more inter-connected than ever before, market volatility is really just a change in degree rather than a fundamental change. In this respect, I think the value investing methodology is just as pertinent and relevant today as it was when I started my career.

"The essence of value investing, to me, is the development of a sense of fairness and integrity because, ultimately, you are looking for a margin of safety by starting off from a point of conservatism. If you do not start off conservatively, you can have a high margin of error, which deviates from being a true value investor. If you look for the downside first, you tend to be more prudent, and this quality helps you form your own opinion rather than following the crowd. Then, when you are not easily swayed by others, you gradually gain a sense of fairness, not just as an investor, but also as a person. This school of thought really helps to develop the right temperament, which indirectly cultivates your investment process and strategy."

For many years, Yeh has woken up at 4:00 A.M. and gone to bed at 8:30 P.M. This disciplined routine began when he worked in New York. At first, it was simply a matter of waking up early to go to work, but then he began to push his limits by waking up slightly earlier each day, which gradually turned into the schedule he keeps today.

Yeh spends the first two hours of the morning clearing out his e-mail inbox, a task he does not enjoy as he has something of an e-mail phobia. Then, with that drudgery out of the way, he heads to the gym for a two-hour physical training session. After reading the daily news, he spends the rest of the day at the office, either meeting with his investment partners or privately thinking and reading about the world.

He modestly explained his current investment strategy: "The way I generate investment ideas today is to be constantly on the lookout for good investment managers who can come up with good ideas. I am fortunate enough to learn from my partners, and since they are smarter than me, I mostly listen, although I occasionally chip in with my viewpoint and insights."

Inviting Yeh to lunch proves an economical exercise because he does not eat lunch. At most, he will order a Diet Coke. At 6:00 P.M. sharp, Yeh returns home to spend time with his family. A wine lover who constantly searches for under-covered boutique wines, he may drink a glass or two before retiring to bed.

Although he is too humble to admit that he is a successful person, Yeh probably would not be able to deny that he is a man of value. Disciplined not only in investing, but also in ensuring his personal well-being, the quote that probably best captures V-Nee Yeh is that of Benjamin Franklin: "Early to bed and early to rise makes a man healthy, wealthy, and wise."

CHAPTER 12

The Accidental Value Investor

Cheah Cheng Hye
Value Partners Group

The unexamined life is not worth living.

—*Socrates*

*C*heah Cheng Hye co-founded Value Partners Limited in 1993. Based in Hong Kong, the asset management company has a mandate to seek underfollowed and out-of-favor investment opportunities in the Asia—Pacific region. Currently serving as chairman and co-chief investment officer, Cheah is responsible for the company's various investment funds and its overall business direction.

Voted among the most influential individuals in the investment business by a number of business magazines, including AsianInvestor and FinanceAsia, Cheah is well on the way to meeting his objective of transforming Value Partners into a world-class investment firm. His dual mission is to introduce and to promote value investing in Asia by constructing an investment process by which ordinary investment teams can achieve extraordinary investment results. The company motto is "Investing through discipline."

The largest asset management company in Asia, with $7.2 billion in total assets under management, Value Partners is also one of only two investment companies listed on a stock exchange in the region. Its flagship fund, Value Partners Classic Fund (A Units), saw a total return of 1,756.4 percent, or 16.9 percent per annum, from inception in April 1993 to December 2011. Its benchmark index, the Hang Seng Index, returned 262.4 percent, or 7.1 percent annually, during the same period.

"I have dedicated myself to lifelong learning," said Cheah Cheng Hye. "When I was 25 years old, I changed my personal signature to 'Learn' because I knew so little about the world and wanted to learn something new each day. In fact, I believe that learning is the only way to become a civilized and responsible human being!"

Having narrowly avoided dropping out of school on several occasions. Cheah appreciates first-hand what a privilege learning is. Born in 1954 in Penang, Malaysia, Cheah was among the poorest of the poor in his early years: "Malaysia was a Third World country when I was growing up, and there was no social safety net to speak of.

"When I was 12 years old, my father passed away after a period of ill health. With no source of income, my family, including my mother and a younger brother and sister, were literally in danger of starving to death. We moved from house to house and regularly faced eviction because we couldn't pay the rent."

As the eldest son, Cheah was forced to go to work to keep his family alive. He recalled: "I sold pineapples on the roadside seven days a week, and I also worked as a hawker selling noodles. School became a part-time leisure activity, and I couldn't even have personal dreams because I was simply clinging on for survival. My mother hoped that I would one day become a clerk so that I wouldn't have to work in the sun."

Cheah aimed a bit higher. Determined to escape from poverty, he studied hard and earned a scholarship to the Penang Free School, an elite secondary school. To avail himself of this learning opportunity, he had to endure a daily 45-minute bicycle ride each way to school. When his bicycle was stolen, he reluctantly had to skip school for a few weeks until an uncle came to his rescue and gave him a used bicycle.

He recalled, "Although my school career was difficult, I had a few claims to fame. I was the junior chess champion at my school, and was considered one of the best young writers in Malaysia. One of my short stories was published in a British magazine, and I wrote a piece on the exploitation of child labor based on my own experiences. After taking my O-level exams at 17, I was forced to leave school and find work to support my family."

As Penang suffered a high unemployment rate in the early 1970s, finding a decent job was not easy. The only opportunity that presented itself in 1971 was a job folding newspapers for the *Star* newspaper, at a salary of 3 Malaysian ringgits per night (equivalent to roughly $1 today). Although he went home each night with his face and hands covered in black ink, Cheah nevertheless considered the job a blessing because he could at least read the news for free.

Three weeks into his new job, Cheah was granted a considerable promotion to trainee reporter. He explained, "The editor of the *Star* found out that I had won some literary prizes during my school years, and so he gave me a chance to become a crime reporter. As no one initially taught me where to look for crime stories, I had to take the initiative. I drove a motorcycle around town, listened to the police radio, and talked to different people to look for leads. Almost half of my stories were based on self-generated ideas and investigations, and my hard work earned me a promotion to subeditor of the *Star* in 1974."

Realizing that his career prospects would be limited if he remained in Malaysia, Cheah began to look farther afield in Asia. When he was offered a sub-editor's position at the *Hong Kong Standard* newspaper in 1974, he accepted without hesitation. In August of that year, Cheah packed his bags, boarded a cargo ship, and set sail toward a new life.

Just 20 years old and with virtually no knowledge of financial markets, Cheah would have been very surprised to hear that he would be managing an investment fund in 19 years' time. He confessed, "Long-term planning was not on my agenda. I drifted from situation to situation, simply responding to opportunities as they arose. My lack of interest in investing at the time is not that surprising: I simply had no money to invest."

After several years at the *Standard*, Cheah joined *Asiaweek* and then moved on to the *Far Eastern Economic Review* and finally *The Asian Wall Street Journal*. Initially he covered a variety of news stories in Hong Kong, but as the city cemented its position as an Asian financial hub, his focus gradually narrowed to economic and business news as his journalism career progressed in the years up to 1989.

To ensure that he could write in-depth and accurate stories, Cheah had no choice but to further his education by reading widely in a variety of areas. He explained: "Having the opportunity to interview prominent political and business figures in Asia gave me deep insight into the region. I learned that business cannot be carried out unless you understand the political, social, historical, and financial aspects involved.

"That realization prompted me to read a lot of history. I was particularly interested in the British Empire, as Hong Kong was then a colony and my home country of Malaysia had once been. I was fascinated with how Britain, a small island nation, had managed to dominate the world for so many years. That in itself is one of the wonders of the world!"

Reading history also equipped Cheah with a better understanding of Asian politics and sparked an interest in finance. He recalled: "After learning about financial modeling and accounting, I came upon *The Money Masters* by John Train, which taught me how good investors invest their money. Although I initially studied these subjects to become a better journalist, in the end I developed a passion for finance and investing."

Whereas an average journalist reacts to an event by researching and then reporting it, an above-average journalist anticipates and prepares for an event before it takes place.

Cheah commented, "What I learned as a journalist also applies to investing. First, good ideas are often self-generated. They come by taking the initiative to learn about new things and by paying attention to detail. Then, it is about prioritizing well and focusing on the main points because much of what we read and hear is pure noise, not useful information. When you are knowledgeable and focused, you are better prepared for whatever events take place. If you are a journalist, then you are able to break the news faster and with greater accuracy than your peers. If you are an investor, then you are able to react more quickly and decisively to opportunities as they arise."

Such knowledge and focus has certainly borne fruit for Cheah. In 1983, when he was with the *Wall Street Journal Asia*, Cheah was the first journalist in Asia to break the news that the Hong Kong dollar would be pegged to the U.S. dollar.

The same year, while investigating the red-hot Hong Kong–based conglomerate Carrian Group, Cheah discovered that the company had incomprehensible accounting practices and was involved in strange dealings with Bank Bumiputra Malaysia. The company soon collapsed amid a chain of dramatic events, including accounting fraud allegations, the suicide of a company advisor, and the murder of a Malaysian bank auditor. Cheah's resulting story in the *Asian Wall Street Journal* was an impressive combination of crime investigation and in-depth analysis of the company's financials.

Throughout 1983 and 1984, Cheah specialized in investigations into banking scandals in Hong Kong, including the collapse of Ka Wah Bank and the Overseas Trust Bank.

In 1986, Cheah carried out an investigation of the Philippines Central Bank and broke the news that it was cooking its books. He also achieved journalistic prominence with his on-the-ground coverage of the "People's Power" revolt on the streets of Manila, which led to the fall of President Ferdinand Marcos.

Cheah said, "After working in journalism for 18 years, I came to the conclusion that I had quite an aptitude for in-depth investment research. Through a friend, I met Mr. Hsieh Fu Hua, then the head of investment bank Morgan Grenfell in Singapore. He asked me whether I would be interested in joining the bank as an investment researcher. With nothing to lose and a desire to try something different, I left journalism and became a stock analyst."

Starting an Investment Hobby Shop

His new career could have had a shaky start. "1989 was a bad year to do anything in Hong Kong because of the Tiananmen Square incident in China," Cheah recalled. "Fortunately, Mr. Hsieh offered me a job as head of equities research. He was interested in setting up a broking division in Hong Kong for Morgan Grenfell, and he needed someone to cover equities.

"In our initial meeting, Mr. Hsieh asked me why he should hire me. I answered that in any business, there is value-added, and then there is 'differentiated' value-added. Although everyone tries to add value to whatever he or she does, I could offer something different thanks to my background in journalism and my research on a wide range of topics. My analysis would offer a different perspective from my competitors. In essence, my expertise was one of a kind."

Cheah noted that finance was a comfortable industry to be in in the 1980s. Bankers and brokers enjoyed long lunches and, in the main, followed only the Hang Seng Index, which consisted of just 33 stocks at the time. Everyone traded in and out of those 33 stocks and made a comfortable living.

Not being comfortable with merely being comfortable, Cheah decided to draw on his unique investment insight and focus on medium- and small-cap companies to distinguish himself from the herd. With his boss's approval, he began his new investment journey.

In addition to generating investment ideas for Morgan Grenfell, Cheah became a proprietary trader for the firm. His ability to analyze the stock market not only from a financial viewpoint but also from historical, political, and social perspectives allowed Cheah to interpret economic reality more accurately than his peers. Accordingly, he generated hefty profits for the firm and received year-end bonuses that exceeded his expectations.

In 1992, Cheah encountered his future business partner, V-Nee Yeh: "V-Nee had returned from the U.S. with the intention of privatizing his family's company, Hsin Chong. As Morgan Grenfell represented the company's minority shareholders, I was responsible for assigning a fair value to the company's worth. Although V-Nee and I represented opposing sides, I came to respect his intelligence and honesty. I knew that if I ever decided to start my own business, he would be a good person to talk to, and even to partner with."

In 1993, Cheah did indeed start thinking about launching his own investment firm. After working at Morgan Grenfell for a few years, and having earned a considerable amount of money, he felt it was time to control his own destiny.

He elaborated: "Honestly, I had become a little fed up with the finance industry and wanted to do my own thing because the industry was, and probably still is, full of what I call 'financial pirates.' These individuals join finance not because they are passionate about investing, but because they have the 'money disease.' Because they think the industry will enable them to make a lot of money, so instead of becoming engineers or lawyers they become bankers. They are a disgrace to human civilization because they contribute nothing!

"If you are a good doctor, you may make a lot of money, but you are probably also adding value in your field. These financial pirates, in contrast, make a lot of money by destroying value and hurting ordinary investors. They are even more dangerous than Somali pirates because they are undetectable. They are well-educated, come from a good background, and dress in nice suits, but they prey on the market by creating and selling investment products that investors shouldn't buy or don't need."

Determined to ward off the money disease, Cheah decided to do his own thing and focus purely on investing: "I knew that if I had the right principles, I wouldn't need to chase money. It would chase me!"

The right principles, for Cheah, led naturally to value investing, with its focus on financial analysis and investment valuation. "I wouldn't be trading in and out of stocks without a valid reason. On the basis of that simple concept, Value Partners was created."

Cheah took his business concept to Yeh, who happened to share the same viewpoint and aspirations, and the two teamed up, officially co-founding Value Partners in Hong Kong in February 1993.

Cheah recalled the early days: "V-Nee and I laugh about it now, but when we started the business it was just me and him and a secretary. We raised $5.6 million, which was basically our own money, and ran the company like a hobby shop. Some people sell collectable toys and model cars; we sell prudent investment analysis and value stocks."

Building a Value Temple

To protect themselves from the money disease and to add real value through individual stock picking, Value Partners focused on small- to mid-cap companies in Hong Kong. This investment strategy allowed the firm to differentiate itself from most of the funds available at that time, which mainly offered investment products that closely tracked the Hang Seng Index.

The two partners quickly settled into well-defined roles. Cheah focused on investment analysis and stock picking, whereas Yeh concentrated on fund raising. "There is a big difference between being a good analyst, a good fund manager, and a good chief executive. Just because you have the skill to analyze investments doesn't mean you have the killer instincts or decisiveness needed to pull the trigger as a fund manager. Even if you are good at both, that still doesn't mean you can raise capital and run an investment fund properly. Fortunately, V-Nee and I teamed up well, and we complement each other."

Cheah believes Yeh to be a rare value investor in Asia today. He explained: "First, he comes from a very good background and has a good network. Second, he understands the difference between value investing on a theoretical Graham-and-Dodd basis and applying that theory realistically and building a business on it. Running a fund is three-dimensional in nature. You have to deal with the structure and maintenance of the fund, you have to deal with clients and employees, and then, of course, you also have to deal with investment analysis and portfolio management.

"I am very fortunate to have a partner like V-Nee, who has managed to traverse the gap between armchair value investor and what I call a master of fund management in a three-dimensional way. He has taken the value investing philosophy and translated it into a solid business model in Asia."

Thanks to Yeh's strong support and Cheah's investment intelligence, Value Partners began to take off in the mid- to late 1990s. As the company began to hire more people, Cheah recognized that he was at the forefront of building a value culture in Asia. To instill the firm's employees with the right spirit and mentality, all newcomers are required to sign an agreement that Cheah calls "My Promise." It is mandatory that all employees frame this agreement, which comprises the following ten cardinal rules, and display it on their desks.

Be honest and straightforward; put my pride, not my ego, into the job; always strive for self-improvement; put clients' interest first; be fair and responsible to shareholders; keep our workplace free from office politics; keep secrets, maintain confidentiality; uphold our reputation for creative high-value solutions; emphasize a user-friendly, cost effective approach; focus on concrete results, not excessive procedure.

Cheah hopes that signing "My Promise" will encourage all of his employees to lead moral and respectable lives. To weed out financial pirates in disguise, he looks for what he calls "learn-ability" and "teach-ability."

He commented, "When I evaluate potential employees, I try to determine whether he or she is learnable and teachable. For example, can they learn new things, and then can they teach what they have learned to others? Sometimes, good students are not good teachers, and vice versa. Scoring high in both categories requires an open mind, humility, and willingness to share.

"When I was a journalist, I started each assignment with a clean sheet of paper. To write a good story, I constantly had to find new ways to improve my 'learn-ability.' Then, because I had to write the story up in an understandable way, I also had to improve my 'teach-ability.' These two concepts are also important in investing."

In building a value temple in Asia, Cheah has instilled Buddhist teachings into the company's culture. Value stocks by their nature tend to underperform the market in the short term because they are usually out of favor or have been overlooked by investors. Cheah often reminds his colleagues of the importance of perseverance and fortitude—basic tenets of the Buddhist faith—in remaining calm in the face of such underperformance.

Also of relevance is the Buddhist emphasis on selflessness. Cheah elaborated: "To build a long-lasting business, it is important to drop one's ego and to let go of the 'self.' In that respect, I would never want Value Partners to become dependent on a particular investment 'star.' Avoiding such dependence requires building an investment process that can be carried out by a group of above-average individuals, and then making sure that process is learnable, teachable, repeatable, scalable, and sustainable.

"Obviously, you need a leader to guide the team, but the overall process has to be carried out by the team. Although each individual on the team may have limitations, teaming up allows each of us to focus on our strengths and maximize our capability. It may sound odd, but my ultimate goal is to industrialize this investment process and turn Value Partners into a factory that produces value investment ideas. We have proven that we can beat the market as a team, so maybe our process is repeatable and transferable."

An Industrialized Process

Cheah noted that the framework underpinning his industrialized investment process originated in the West, where its proponents include such well-known value investors as Benjamin Graham and Warren

Buffett. His own contribution to the process has been to adjust its concepts to render them more applicable to the Asian environment.

In formulating investment ideas, Cheah and his team look for the three Rs: the right business operated by the right people and selling at the right price. In the process, they think as contrarians and divide the Asian stock universe into three categories:

1. Undervalued and out-of-favor stocks
2. Fairly valued and highly recommended stocks
3. Overvalued concept stocks

He explained, "Our main job is to invest in stocks in the first category and perhaps in those that fall between the first and second. Sell-side analysts tend to recommend a lot of Category 2 stocks, which we are always skeptical about. As for Category 3 stocks, they are the ones recommended by the media and taxi drivers. We aim to buy Category 1 stocks consistently and wait for them to become Category 2 stocks. When they begin to approach Category 3, we sell."

Although this approach may sound simple in theory, in practice it can be rather challenging. Cheah noted, "No Asian investor likes to stick his or her neck out and buy an unpopular item. Unlike the American stock market, which has ample liquidity, undervalued stocks in Asia can have zero volume on a trading day, and so the buying and selling process can be painful."

After categorizing stocks in this manner and preliminarily looking at the valuation of those of interest, the next step is in-depth research into the underlying businesses. Cheah and his team have standardized their valuation model and comparison metric to allow them to compare stocks within and across industries quantitatively. In the 1990s, Benjamin Graham's *Security Analysis* served as the team's reference book, but since then they have been using Martin Fridson's *Financial Statement Analysis: A Practitioner's Guide*.

Cheah elaborated: "We are increasingly focused on qualitative research rather than quantitative analysis because in Asia, stocks that are selling cheap are likely to be in a lousy business, that is, they are nothing but what Graham calls 'cigar butt' stocks that have only a few puffs left. Even if bought at a good discount, these businesses can still go under because they lack sustainability and competitive advantage."

Cheah said that Value Partners now focuses on business strength and core competence, and the firm's team of analysts visits as many as 2,500 companies a year, kicking tires to distinguish the good from the bad.

Once an opportunity has been identified, Cheah and his team carefully deliberate before making an investment decision. "I think decision-making is often neglected as a process because when it comes to investing, someone has to pull the trigger," he said.

"Oftentimes if you were to ask a team of finance professors to actually pull the trigger on a billion-dollar decision, they probably couldn't because they are too academic," Cheah continued. "And sometimes as an analyst, even if you know you are theoretically correct, you are still afraid to make a decision because you don't want to be blamed if things turn out wrong. I call this a lack of killer instinct.

"To avoid that kind of indecision, we never blame anyone for making an investment mistake. However, that doesn't mean we make decisions casually. Instead, by applying Buddhist teaching on removing the 'self' from the equation, we let go of our egos and do not worry about what others will think of us if we turn out to be wrong. Then, as we focus purely on the facts, we come up with an objective decision."

That said, Cheah emphasized that "we are far from being invincible. We do make mistakes! In fact, analysis of our decision-making process since 1993 shows that we have made the wrong decision about one-third of the time, with another third of our decisions neither right nor wrong and another third spot on. To outperform the market, we must minimize our losses on mistakes by constantly monitoring our portfolio and distinguishing the good and bad stocks within it."

In this respect, Cheah likes to paraphrase Socrates: "Those who know know they know nothing; and those who know they don't know know everything." Humility will get you farther in the investment game than pretending to be intelligent.

In his early days as a fund manager, Cheah believed in having a very concentrated portfolio, but later he came to the conclusion that a diversified portfolio makes more sense. He explained, "At first, I was proud to have a concentrated portfolio of around 30 to 40 stocks, but then I began to realize that there are simply too many crooks out there who sound and look convincing, but end up cheating us as shareholders.

"In addition, there are numerous external forces affecting companies in Asia, whether they be business, economic, or politics driven. To protect ourselves from losses, it is wiser to have a diversified portfolio in which no single stock accounts for more than 2 percent."

When Value Partners was still relatively small, it invested by buying stocks outright in the open market. As the firm's total assets under management grew, however, buying the stocks of small- to mid-sized companies became virtually impossible due to the limited liquidity in the open market. The liquidity issue, in fact, got Cheah into trouble.

In December 1998, the Hong Kong Securities and Futures Commission (SFC) publicly reprimanded Value Partners and Cheah for placing a number of buy orders on five stocks before the close of the trading day, thereby artificially inflating their closing prices. The SFC released a statement that read: "Although unintentional, Cheah should have known that trading in this manner had the potential to affect the closing prices of the stocks and could therefore have been prejudicial to the integrity of the market."

Cheah explained: "It is impossible today to explain how difficult it was to have a portfolio specializing in small-cap stocks in the 1993 to 1999 period. These stocks were like private equity, and there were days on which they had no trading volume at all. Then came the financial crisis of 1997, and toward the end of 1998 there were months in which every possible buyer and seller of our stocks had simply disappeared. We tried to create a market by either buying or selling a security until we hit a counterparty, but there were none.

"To the general public, we appeared to be engaging in price manipulation, but what actually happened was much simpler than that. In any case, I took full responsibility and explained the reasons for our actions to the SFC. Although they accepted them, they were not satisfied and gave us a warning."

Having learned his lesson, Cheah revised the firm's investment process by adding a specialized team of stock dealers to facilitate investment trades. Moreover, as Value Partners had become quite a large company by local standards, Cheah decided that taking positions on small companies required a different approach.

He said, "We can easily buy 5 to 10 percent of a small company these days. To leverage on our size and reputation, we often structure a deal to buy a single block of shares directly from the company rather than buying it on the open market. In American terms, this is known as private investment in public equities, or PIPES for short. The beauty of this kind of transaction is that we can buy at a discounted market price or structure a convertible bond with the company."

Once this has been accomplished, Cheah and his team monitor their investment positions closely. Adding a journalistic element to the exercise, Cheah asks his colleagues to imagine what the newspaper headlines on their holdings would be. He elaborated: "I like to ask my team to visualize the future, to imagine what journalists will write about the company in three months or a year. In response, they will often simply consult the price chart. But I don't want that. I want a true visualization of the future!"

A Value March Forward

Reflecting on his years at Value Partners, Cheah believes that the most memorable event in the company's history occurred between 2001 and 2002 when its total assets under management reached the $1 billion mark.

He recalled, "There was a bit of disunity on the team at the time because some people wanted to close the fund and keep the company small, whereas others wanted to grow the company to show the world that an Asian asset management company could raise serious money and be sustainable. I happened to be on the side of those who wanted to pursue growth.

"The debate went on for months. Although I agreed that the selling point of an asset management company is its performance, not its size, I eventually won the debate, not because I was the co-founder of the firm but because we, as a team, had created a thorough investment process whose application allowed us to form small units within the firm in a kind of military formation.

"Doing so permitted us to retain a small unit culture while becoming large as a whole. Today, we have around six units, each of which has five to six members managing their own fund. These units are semi-autonomous. Hence, their members do not feel like they are working for a big company, and so are still hungry, passionate, and innovative. Our motto is 'Small enough to be effective, big enough to be strong!'"

In Cheah's position as chairman and co-chief investment officer of Value Partners, providing leadership and direction requires an extra skill set: macro analysis.

Cheah elaborated: "As the leader of the company, I must constantly learn new strategies and ideas to take the company to the next level. Not only do I have to consider the structure of the company, but also how we can evolve as a whole in line with the broader macro environment. If we had decided to close the fund and remain a small entity in the early 2000s, we would basically have been ignoring the growth potential in Asia and the macro landscape. Without progress, you fall behind.

"As diehard bottom-up value investors, we focus on businesses. But at my level, I must also pay attention to top-down factors, such as the state and outlook of the economy so that I can guide my team in asset and portfolio allocation. For example, if you know that the economy is softening, you need to increase your cash holdings or at least allocate your positions to more defensive sectors. You cannot simply focus on a company and ignore the surrounding environment!"

Although some would view him as a workaholic, Cheah is a ferocious reader who never stops learning. In addition to reading, which is both a hobby and a means of relaxation, Cheah, a practicing Buddhist, also meditates for about forty minutes a day. Meditating not only allows him to unwind, but to set his mind free and to observe it from the inside, no doubt generating a few investment ideas.

Cheah believes that his success is partly due to simple luck. He happened to be in the right place at the right time when China began to open up its economy in December 1978 and Deng Xiaoping announced the country's Open Door Policy to promote market forces and a capitalist-inclined system. Then, in 1992 during his southern China tour, Deng pronounced that "to get rich is glorious!" Until his death in 1997, Deng was a strong advocate of the "four modernizations" originally set forth in the 1960s to strengthen agriculture, industry, national defense, and science and technology.

Marching forward with his team at Value Partners, Cheah would add a fifth modernization: financial market modernization. He concluded, "China has gone through traumatic times, particularly in the nineteenth and twentieth centuries. It was once considered the 'sick man of Asia.' Although the country has recently exceeded our wildest expectations in terms of economic development, poverty eradication, and urbanization, in many respects its financial system remains in its infancy.

"In the years to come, China will develop a world-class financial industry, and that is where Value Partners and the Hong Kong people come in. We can help contribute to this fifth modernization. The rising wealth of the Chinese people makes them vulnerable to the financial pirates lurking out there. Our mission is to protect them by showing them the benefits of value investing."

CHAPTER 13

The Making of a Value Investor

If you can keep your head when all about you
Are losing theirs and blaming it on you;
If you can trust yourself when all men doubt you,
But make allowance for their doubting too;
If you can wait and not be tired by waiting;
If you can meet with triumph and disaster
And treat those imposters just the same;
If you can talk with crowds and keep your virtue,
Or walk with kings—nor lose the common touch,
If neither foes nor loving friends can hurt you,
If all men count with you, but none too much;
Yours is the Earth and everything that's in it,
And—which is more—you'll be a Man!

—*Rudyard Kipling*

I once asked Donald Keough, former president of Coca-Cola, what it takes to become a good leader. He replied that leaders come in different shapes and sizes, and that it is difficult to predict who will become a good one. Writing this book led me to believe that his comment is equally applicable to investing. Good investors come in different shapes and sizes, and there is no strict rule for identifying whose approach is best.

V-Nee Yeh of Value Partners in Hong Kong told me that many investors and investment books like to discuss the "right" investment style. Yet he believes it is more appropriate to first understand one's temperament and compatibility and then to choose a style. "If you are a calm and patient person, then the value investing approach may be right for you, but if you are jumpy and aggressive, then a more trading-oriented style may be more suitable."

Value investing is the focus of this book. Although I certainly do not rule out the possibility that other forms of investing may work, my encounters with 12 successful investors from around the world have convinced me that value investing works in a variety of countries, and that the philosophy underpinning it is as applicable today as it was when Benjamin Graham first began promoting it in the 1920s.

During the course of researching and writing this book, I have made several observations about what it means, and what it takes, to be a value investor. This concluding chapter summarizes those observations.

A Humble Portfolio Construction

"Humble" is probably the best word to characterize the value investors featured in this book. Although humility is a virtue in its own right, in investing it translates into the margin of safety concept, which defends against uncertainty.

Jean-Marie Eveillard considers humility to be an essential require-ment for investment success. The quality allows investors to be aware that they are far from being invincible, and that they can be wrong at times: "I acknowledge the fact that I am uncertain about the future, so my priority is to avoid losing money, rather than to generate big returns."

Eveillard added that by assigning a margin of safety to investments, investors also need patience to wait for their ideas to play out. As Benjamin Graham said, "In the short run, the market is a voting machine, but in the long run, it is a weighing machine."

Humility not only encourages investors to look for a margin of safety, it also equips them with open minds. As Mark Mobius put it, "With an open mind, you can accept that the world changes and that you must constantly learn new things to keep pace with it."

Knowing that the world can be uncertain, most value investors featured in this book hold diversified portfolios. Generating superior investment performance is certainly an important aim, but safeguarding investors' assets and protecting them from losses is just as crucial. In that sense, diversification is a natural course of action.

It is important to distinguish here the major difference between risk and uncertainty. Risk involves an unknown outcome that can be calculated or defined. For example, playing poker or investing in a stock can be risky, but people always know their odds and possible losses.

Uncertainty, in contrast, implies an unknown outcome that cannot be calculated or identified. For example, no one has the perfect foresight to predict the duration of a market correction or an economic recession. Although the market is uncertain, investors can nevertheless calculate the risk of their investments quantitatively.

In essence, value investors diversify their portfolios not because their investments are deemed risky, but because they acknowledge that the world is uncertain. William Browne believes that diversification is the only way to hedge against such an uncertainty: "Some investors ask us why we would rather diversify into our twenty-fifth stock rather than put that money into our ten best holdings. The truth is, we really aren't certain enough to say which are our ten best, and so we would rather diversify."

Warren Buffett is famous for running a concentrated portfolio. Although the late Walter Schloss agreed that it would be easier to keep a concentrated portfolio, he took a more cautious approach in his investment career: "I see that there are many people trying to be like Warren, but they should take note that he is not only a good analyst; he is also a good judge of people and businesses. I know my limitations, so I'd rather invest in the way I am most comfortable with."

Diversification is almost mandatory in emerging economies. Due to the economic and political instability in many countries, good businesses come and go, and even the most sophisticated investors can be cheated.

Hong Kong–based Cheah Cheng Hye told me: "At first, I was proud to have a concentrated portfolio, but then I began to realize that there are simply too many crooks out there who sound and look convincing, but end up cheating us as shareholders."

To a certain extent, diversification is a matter of degree. For example, London-based Anthony Nutt holds 100 to 110 stocks in his investment funds, but the top 10 holdings usually account for 40 percent of his portfolios.

More selective with his investments, Singapore-based Teng Ngiek Lian holds roughly 30 stocks. He said that a more concentrated portfolio allows him to focus on surer bets and to devote more time and expertise to businesses that he knows well.

Although Teng considers his portfolio holdings to be concentrated, 30 is still quite a high number of stocks to hold. In *A Random Walk Down Wall Street*, Burton Malkiel notes that when a portfolio contains roughly 20 equally sized and well-diversified stocks, the total risk is reduced by roughly 70 percent. By spreading his holdings across the Asia—Pacific region, Teng has actually reduced the amount of country-, political-, and business-specific risk.

The Art of Valuation

By reading finance books or taking investment valuation classes, anyone can come up with a fair valuation of an investment. The difficult part, then, lies in qualitative analysis because good value investors have the experience and know-how to predict the sustainability and durability of businesses.

Spanish value investor Francisco Paramés claims to use nothing more sophisticated than a calculator for investment analysis. He believes that "it is not how sophisticated you are in your valuation model, but how well you know the business and how well you assess its competitive advantage."

Similarly, Jean-Marie Eveillard prefers simple investment measures because coming up with the intrinsic value of a business is a rough estimate, never a precise figure. If investors build sophisticated investment models that deduce the worth of a business down to the penny, they are probably trying too hard.

The important point here is that intrinsic value is a numeric range that fluctuates over time. As the world changes, the critical factor is how investors qualitatively assess business and economic conditions and adjust their calculation accordingly.

After he retired in 2006, Eveillard taught value investing at Columbia University. He noticed that many students thought qualitative analysis involved pages of intensive writing and explanation. He explained, "What I tried to stress to them was that they needed to think hard and then list no more than three to four strengths and weaknesses of the business."

Qualitative analysis sometimes goes beyond pure thinking. It requires action. The privilege of being an investment professional is that one is often able to meet company management. Thomas Kahn of Kahn Brothers told me, "We always ask ourselves what the catalysts are that can turn around undervalued companies. In determining these catalysts, I like to talk to management, assess their abilities and personalities, and understand their way of thinking so that we are on the same page."

Constantly traveling to the most exotic countries to look for the next investment opportunity, Mark Mobius cautions that the financial numbers in emerging markets are not entirely trustworthy: "You have to talk to company management, look into their eyes, and determine whether they are reliable."

Reading for Ideas

People often ask how successful value investors come up with their investment ideas. The simple answer is that they read a great deal.

Francisco Paramés argues that idea generation comes from having a "consistent understanding of the world and synchronizing it with all of the information you have accumulated." It is a disciplined process because it does not happen by waking up one day and recklessly looking for ideas. For that matter, the desire to learn new subjects and the willingness to keep an open mind are critical.

Thomas Kahn claims not to know any good investors who do not read. His father, Irving, is a good example: "My father has read thousands of books, and has a special interest in science. Because of his vast knowledge of the subject, he focuses on the future and rarely dwells on the past. He constantly looks forward to the technological break-throughs and good things that will happen to mankind in the future."

Irving Kahn himself reminisced about the early days when investors needed the right investment principles and mindset to generate investment ideas. Now, with the widespread use of the Internet, finding good investment ideas has become easier.

He told me, "There were only a handful of industries in which to look for stocks in the old days. Now there are so many different types of businesses in so many different countries that investors can easily find something. Besides, the Internet has made more information available. If you complain that you cannot find opportunities, then that means you either haven't looked hard enough or you haven't read broadly enough!"

In Asia, Cheah Cheng Hye has dedicated himself to lifelong learning. He believes that good ideas are often self-generated. They come from paying attention to detail and patiently waiting for events to take place. Cheah takes a creative approach by asking his investment team to visualize the future of their investments by imagining what journalists will write about them in a year's time.

Some people attribute good investment ideas to pure luck, but they should pay heed to what the Roman philosopher Seneca wrote many years ago: "Luck is when preparation meets opportunity!"

More than Just the Fundamentals

There is a common perception that value investors focus purely on the fundamentals of businesses and disregard the broader economy. Although this may be the case in more developed economies, those who invest in emerging markets tend to keep an eye on macro factors. As Cheah Cheng Hye said, "You cannot simply focus on a company and ignore the surrounding environment."

In Singapore, Teng Ngiek Lian believes that an understanding of Asian politics is particularly important. Because a change in political wind can lead to a drastic change in the economic direction of a region, opportunities come and go quickly.

As Asia's shorter economic cycle often leads to greater market volatility than that of mature economies, value investing should be applied in a more flexible manner than what Benjamin Graham or Warren Buffett has preached in the West.

Teng cautioned, "Stocks can swing wildly. A long-term buy-and-hold strategy without due regard to market volatility can lead to underperformance. This is not to say that one should actively trade the market, but it is wise for investors to make a profit when the market is euphoric or a stock has reached its full valuation, and then to buy again when the market corrects."

Japan's deflationary environment during the 1990s taught Shuhei Abe of the SPARX Group the importance of taking a broader view and adapting to the situation at hand. Abe also suggests that investors must make adjustments to practice value investing in their respective countries.

To cope with the Lost Decade in Japan, Abe came to the conclusion that knowing which investments are undervalued also means knowing which are overvalued. To benefit from both, he created a long-short investment strategy.

With his new approach, even when Japan's economy continued to fall, Abe's investments thrived. He told me, "To continue to bring Japanese market solutions to investors, we had to evolve. We had to build new trading skills that would allow us to fulfill clients' real needs— to preserve capital and generate positive returns."

American and European value investors have also paid more attention to economic and political policies in recent years, especially since the fall of Lehman Brothers.

Jean-Marie Eveillard is unsure whether we are still in a post–World War II economic and financial landscape or if we have been more influenced by the financial crisis of 2008. He warns fellow value investors to be bottom-up all they want, but always keep an eye on the top-down.

In the United Kingdom, Anthony Nutt remains a firm believer in the bottom-up approach. However, he agrees with Eveillard that macroeconomic policies have had great impacts on global stock markets over the past few years: "By looking at these policies with a top-down view, my job is also to identify long-term business trends. As long as we choose the right sector, we think that good companies with varying degrees of success can do well in different economic cycles."

All of the value investors I interviewed have acquired in-depth industry and business knowledge over long periods. Although their investment rationale has always been based on the bottom-up approach, they grasp broad economic topics very well. They are not concerned about whether inflation is 2 or 2.5 percent, or whether the unemployment rate is 8 or 8.5 percent, but their overall macroeconomic framework and understanding complements their bottom-up investment analysis.

Timing for an Exit

The value investors in this book tend to have investment horizons of at least three to five years. When choosing the time to sell, they focus more heavily on investment valuation than on the investment's holding period.

For Anthony Nutt, the most difficult aspect of investing is not determining whether a stock is cheap or expensive, but determining whether other investors are identifying the very same stock. If a stock is overlooked by the general market, it can stay undervalued for a while. To reduce any time-related anxiety, Nutt times his exit based on investment valuation. He sells his investments only when they have become fully valued, or their business conditions begin to deteriorate.

Like Nutt, Irving and Thomas Kahn shun investment time frames. Some of their holdings have been in their portfolios for decades. They said that investors must avoid shortsightedness when holding value stocks because patience and discipline are paramount.

The Kahns note that failure of a stock to rise within a few months or years does not necessarily mean that it is a non-performer. Value stocks often lag behind the general market for the majority of their holding period. When their true worth is finally recognized, investors are often surprised at their attractive annualized investment returns relative to the broader market.

In value investing, there is such a thing as the "value trap," when a stock that has been beaten down is mistaken for a value stock. Jean-Marie Eveillard believes that if a stock is a real value deal, and if people still call it a "trap," then it is their own problem: "You can't say that it is a trap just because your holding period is mismatched with the time it takes for the stock to recover. If you have patience, and if your analysis is right, then the market will acknowledge the stock eventually!"

However, Eveillard believes that there is a difference between a "temporary unrealized capital loss" and "permanent capital impairment." The former requires patience because the value stock needs time to recover. The latter means the investor has misjudged the strengths and weaknesses of a business. When this happens, one should quickly cut the loss, learn from the mistake, and move on.

In emerging markets, timing for an exit requires a contrarian mindset. Mark Mobius has a minimum holding period of five years, within which he welcomes market swings. "Emerging markets are somewhat immature, and people get overly bullish and bearish all of the time. By focusing on value, we get in when everyone else is trying to get out. Also, our value discipline lets us compare different markets to see which ones are overpriced, so by the time everyone is trying to get in, we are getting out," he explained.

Long-term investment performance comes from two returns: return on investments and the compounding effect of reinvestments. Many investors brag about their superior return on a particular investment. The trouble is, do they have more of these investments lined up?

V-Nee Yeh in Hong Kong always considers reinvestment risk when he sells his holdings: "Most people under-price and under-analyze the reinvestment risk. Even if you make a good investment and sell it, eventually you have to reinvest that money. The real distinction between a good and average investor is that the former constantly has good ideas about reinvesting capital to create a compounding effect."

Super-investor Walter Schloss, who focused more on the numbers than on the potential of businesses, always sold his holdings too early when they reached a reasonable price. Because he focused on the downside risk, he neglected the potential upside. In the end, he had to outwork his peers to come up with reinvestment ideas.

Schloss commented, "Sometimes in life you cannot regret things that didn't work out or that could have worked out better. The challenge in life is knowing what's next. After all, my goal was to keep losses down, and if I could catch a few stocks going up, compound returns would work their magic."

Although Schloss was too humble to admit it, even selling too soon generated a compound return of 16 percent per annum for over 46 years. Compared to the Standard & Poor 500s return of roughly 10 percent over the same period, investing with Schloss would have generated ten times more money.

Having the Right Temperament

My discussions with the 12 investors convinced me that being a value investor is highly dependent on character. Jean-Marie Eveillard asked, "How come there are so few value investors out there?" His answer was that they had to accept lagging behind their peers and that they would suffer psychologically and financially in doing so.

Knowing that there is no instant gratification in an investment, V-Nee Yeh thinks that the value investing philosophy boils down to character. Value investing attracts conservative people who look for the downside risk of an investment first.

He told me, "Value investing is the development of a sense of fairness because ultimately you are looking for a margin of safety by starting off from a point of conservatism. By doing so it encourages prudence and guards against following the crowd. This school of thought helps develop the right temperament, which indirectly cultivates an investment process and strategy."

William Browne believes that investors are naturally emotional and affected by the news, but value investors can still maintain their calm in face of opinions and comments from the media. Perhaps the secret is their intellectual framework for thinking objectively.

All of these value investors believe that investing is half art and half science. Although we need the basics to calculate the value of an investment, the more important part is to think hard. As Thomas Kahn said, if the investment game were all about numbers, computer programs would be able to find the right stock all the time. The truth is that they cannot.

As I learned when writing my last book, *Behind the Berkshire Hathaway Curtain: Lessons from Warren Buffett's Top Business Leaders*, an investment decision should always be based on clear facts and assumptions because a business can only be worth so much. As Buffett said, "Price is what you pay, value is what you get."

A superior investment track record is not just about a year or two of outperformance. It is about surviving the market under various circumstances. Having the right investment model is important, but investing with honesty and integrity are more critical. The late Walter Schloss, who endured 18 economic recessions in his long life of 95 years, is a role model for every investor.

Warren Buffett said of Schloss in a statement after his death in February 2012: "He had an extraordinary investment record, but even more important, he set an example for integrity in investment management. Walter never made a dime off of his investors unless they themselves made significant money. He charged no fixed fee at all and merely shared in their profits. His fiduciary sense was every bit the equal of his investment skills."

William Browne said that Schloss was packed with integrity because he never came close to any unclean dealings, and his responsibility had always been to protect investors from losses. Browne said, "Friends and clients may forgive you for the silly mistakes you make in the stock market, but never for a dishonest mistake!"

Always optimistic about the future and never allowing stress to get in his way, Schloss's dear friend Irving Kahn would argue that wealth with no health means nothing.

At 106 years of age, Kahn thinks that the key ingredient to successful investing, not just for the value investor but for every investor, is to stay in motion, meet different people, be inspired, read a lot, and focus on the future: "There is always something to do. You just need to look harder, be creative, and be a little flexible!"

All in all, investing should be fun and challenging, not stressful and worrying. In an uncertain world, the practice of value investing is really a way to maintain a peaceful mind-set. By focusing on a margin of safety, thinking for the long term, and having patience, the goal is to achieve investment stability over time. In the process, investors may well achieve happiness and satisfaction in life.

Benjamin Graham, the father of value investing, should have the last word: "The investor's chief problem—and even his worst enemy—is likely to be himself."

Acknowledgments

This book is a team effort. In fact, I see myself more as organizer and coordinator than author. Without my publisher, John Wiley & Sons, the book would never have come into existence, and without the collective participation of the many respected value investors, there would be no book to publish.

I would first like to thank Irving Kahn, Mark Mobius, Jean-Marie Eveillard, Thomas Kahn, William Browne, Teng Ngiek Lian, Anthony Nutt, Shuhei Abe, Cheah Cheng Hye, V-Nee Yeh, and Francisco García Paramés for their participation and valuable contributions. Interviewing them was an honor, and I can think of no better way of discovering the essence of value investing than learning directly from them and their collective experience.

Walter Schloss passed away on February 19, 2012, in Manhattan, New York. He was 95 years old. I remember the day I spoke to him in late September 2011, when he agreed to be featured in this book. On the phone, he told me about his travel plans, so a better time to meet would be in early 2012. He said, however, that if we could meet before his travels, it would work.

Without hesitation, I flew to New York from Hong Kong to meet Walter. Visiting his apartment in Manhattan and spending an entire morning with him, I learned about the meaning of success and the concepts of value investing. More important, I learned about honesty and integrity. At the end of our meeting, he mentioned how much he loves America because the country has given him the opportunity to do what he enjoys most: investing. Meeting the man was certainly an honor.

In addition to interviewing all of these investing legends, many individuals assisted me on my journey, for which I am most grateful. They include Matthew Kubo, Andrew Kahn, Beltrán Parages Revertera, Hedda Nadler, Robert Crawshaw, Javier Sáenz De Cenzano, Richard Piliero, Debbie Lusman, Alicia Wyllie, Biddy Hung, Anne Lui, Lisa Griffith, Judy Larson, and Zita Ng.

Bruce Greenwald, academic director of the Heilbrunn Center for Graham & Dodd Investing at Columbia University, was kind enough to write the foreword to the book. The *New York Times* has described him as "a guru to Wall Street's gurus," so Professor Greenwald's contribution certainly adds weight to my work.

Besides Professor Greenwald, many prominent figures directly and indirectly encouraged my writing effort. They include Donald Keough, Warren Buffett, Donald Yacktman, David Darst, Nate Dalton, Charles Mak, and Prem Jain.

After publishing my first book, *Behind the Berkshire Hathaway Curtain: Lessons from Warren Buffett's Top Business Leaders*, I assumed my writing career was over and that I would be a one-book author. However, the positive feedback I received from my publisher and from readers around the world encouraged me to keep writing.

As the first book concerned Warren Buffett, one of the world's best-known value investors, and the factors underpinning the success of his associates, it was only natural that my second book should focus on value investing. Interviewing renowned value investors from around the world was the obvious course of action, and *The Value Investors: Lessons from the World's Top Fund Managers* is the result.

Although coming up with the subject of my second book was not difficult, formulating a list of prominent value investors presented more of a challenge. The United States is home to many legendary value investors, but I wanted the book to be as culturally diverse as possible to reveal why individuals from different parts of the world share a similar investment mindset. Many people gave me general support and also helped me to brainstorm ideas, and sincere thanks are particularly due to Brian Lui, William Tsang, Kit Chan, Ambrose Tong, Michael Wong, Joyce Tsang, Tristan Wan, Dennis Lam, Tommy Jim, Bonnie Chan, Claire Chan, Sharon Chow, Darrin Woo, Jonathan Hui, Terence Hsu, and Dev Sujanani.

John Wiley & Sons gave its full support to this book, and I would like to thank Nick Wallwork, Jules Yap, Gemma Rosey Diaz, and Stefan Skeen for their help in the publication process. I would also like to thank Debra Englander, without whose guidance at the beginning of my writing career I would never have become a published author in the first place.

Although I am responsible for the flow and structure of the book, my personal editors, Erika Hebblethwaite, Mike Poole, and Nick Case, have helped me to perfect my use of the English language. The beauty of having both female and male editors is that they provide a good balance of feminine and masculine perspectives.

Last, but not least, I would like to thank my family for their support, including my wife, Jacinth, my daughter, Chelsea, my late father, Yat-San, my mother, Mylene, my sister, Jade, and my brother-in-law, Johnson.

When I began this project, my mother was worried about how I would find the time and luxury to write a book while dealing with a difficult economy, raising a family, and running an asset management company. My secret, I told her, is consistency. The book comprises 13 chapters, and each chapter contains roughly 5,000 words. I assured her that if I spent just one hour a day writing 500 words—just 500 words—then I could comfortably finish the book in five months with plenty of time left over to fulfill my other responsibilities.

I learned something similar from my interviewees. Superior investment performance, and respect from one's peers, does not come from a year or two of good returns. It is delivering sustainable investment returns consistently that counts!

As I wrote at the start, this book has not been an individual endeavor but is the result of a team effort. I could never have turned my dream into reality without the contribution of everyone mentioned here. Thank you all!

About the Author

Ronald W. Chan is the founder of Chartwell Capital Limited, an investment management company based in Hong Kong. He is a frequent contributor to financial newspapers and magazines in the Asia−Pacific region, and is the author of *Behind the Berkshire Hathaway Curtain: Lessons from Warren Buffett's Top Business Leaders*. Chan received bachelor of science degrees in finance and accounting from the Stern School of Business at New York University.

Index